D0563289

# FINDING GOD IN TROUBLED TIMES

*The Holy Spirit and Suffering*

Richard J. Hauser, S.J.

**PAULIST PRESS** • New York / Mahwah, N.J.

ACKNOWLEDGMENTS

The Publisher gratefully acknowledges use of the following materials: excerpts from *The Death of Ivan Ilyich* by Leo Tolstoy, translated by Lynn Solotaroff, translation copyright © 1981 by Bantam, a division of Bantam Doubleday Dell Publishing Group, Inc. Used by permission of Bantam Doubleday Dell Publishing Group, Inc.; excerpts reprinted from *God and Human Suffering* by Douglas John Hall, copyright © 1986 Augsburg Publishing House. Used by permission of Augsburg Fortress; excerpts from *God and Human Anguish* by S. Paul Schilling, copyright © 1977 by Abingdon Press.

Library of Congress Cataloging-in-Publication Data

Hauser, Richard J.
    Finding God in troubled times : the Holy Spirit and suffering / Richard J. Hauser.
        p.   cm.
    Includes bibliographical references.
    ISBN 0-8091-3531-0 (paper)
    1. Suffering—Religious aspects—Christianity.   2. Holy Spirit.   I. Title.
    BT732.7.H39   1994
    231'.8—dc20                                                                                94-30152
                                                                                                        CIP

Published by Paulist Press
997 Macarthur Boulevard
Mahwah, New Jersey 07430

Printed and bound in the
United States of America

# CONTENTS

*To my Creighton students
for sharing their sufferings
and so making this book possible*

# I. WHERE IS GOD IN SUFFERING?

Several years ago six students at our university were killed in two auto accidents, all within two months. In the first accident a drunken driver plowed his car through a group of forty students on a remote rural road. Two were killed; several maimed; several knocked unconscious. Help was some time in coming. In the interim fellow students attempted to restore life to the dying by mouth to mouth resuscitation and to give emergency first aid to the maimed and unconscious. Later that night many arrived in my dorm room stunned and spattered with blood.

In the second accident a drunken driver swerved from his lane into a van carrying seven of our students. The van, forced off the interstate highway, rolled down a deep embankment. Five students were thrown from the car. Four died within twenty-four hours. The university community was traumatized; we had not recovered from the first accident. Now this.

We are a religiously sponsored university. Our mission statement commits us to providing a Christian faith environment conducive to integrating all aspects of university life with religious belief. Coping with these tragedies now became crucial for this faith. Students whose faith had never been so challenged were asking: How could God do this to us? The question became more poignant because each of the deceased was known as a good person.

How could God do this to us? Our responses seemed to fall into three categories; each presumed that God was the direct cause of our suffering. First and most common: "God's plan is perfect, but God's ways are not our ways. While on earth we will never understand the mysterious ways of God's Providence; only in heaven we will understand."

The second response: "God's plan is perfect; God is trying to teach us something. Something good will come from the accidents and then we will understand God's purpose for sending our suffering."

The third response, "God is punishing us for our wrongdoing. We must examine our lives to discover what we have done to deserve this." The first two responses I observed most frequently in public attempts to provide consolation — especially during the funeral homilies. The third was usually confided to me privately by individuals who feared that God may be punishing them for some misdeed.

I became increasingly uncomfortable with two fundamental assumptions underlying these responses. First, all shared an assumption about God's relationship to this world. They assumed that God is the direct cause of all that happens in this world, and, therefore, that God had directly caused the automobile accidents resulting in the deaths of our students. Were we to conclude that God had used the drivers of the automobiles to execute Providence? I wondered how these unfortunate individuals and their families and friends felt about being used this way by God! And if God is the direct cause of this suffering, isn't God likewise the direct cause of all the world's suffering: accidents and disease, floods and droughts, wars and starvation, murders and rapes?

Second, all shared an assumption about the human relationship to God, an assumption equally troubling to me. All assumed that human freedom and responsibility is limited by God's plan. They implied that to some degree we human beings are passive instruments in the hands of a God who controls our life through an intractable Providence. Does this mean that the appropriate human response to all that happens in life is to humble ourselves and accept without questions whatever happens as part of God's plans? Doesn't this impinge upon human freedom and dignity? Are we really just puppets in the hands of the Almighty?

Where was God in our suffering? We were confused: how could a God who claims to act toward us as a loving Father cause such suffering? One mother of a deceased student shared her confusion with me. As a parent she could not grasp how a Father-God could act this way. To her it was incompatible with the notion of parenthood.

I knew many of the deceased well; one was a neighbor on my dorm floor. So for me the weeks after the accidents were marked by students streaming in to see me day and night. I was exhausted from the emotional strain and from the lack of sleep due to the late night counseling sessions — many students experienced weeks of insomnia. But I was even more exhausted by my efforts to say something that would help process the grief. I admired our students for making faith so central in processing their grief. I felt that if their faith could make it through this, it could make it through anything. I felt good that our religiously sponsored institution was succeeding in its effort to provide a faith atmosphere for integrating life. And all the more I wanted to help.

I realized during this time that I myself had not adequately thought through my own belief about God's relationship to suffering. It was during this period that the idea of writing a book first occurred.

### Religion and Suffering

Before dealing specifically with the Christian tradition, it is helpful to set our discussion in a wider context with some general reflections on religion and suffering. Two notes on my terminology are important. I use the term *religion* to refer to belief systems that assume the existence of a transcendent reality — God — with whom believers can relate in some way. And I use the term *suffering* to refer to *any* perceived disorder, be the disorder major or minor. Clearly the accidents described above were major disorders and perceived by all as such. Most human sufferings are less momentous. Baldness — if I may use a personal example — is, in comparison, quite minor. However, to the degree that it is perceived as a disorder, it qualifies as a suffering.

Religions have a crucial role in helping believers deal with suffering. Sociologists who analyze societal institutions in terms of their functions advise us that each institution flourishes to the extent that it fulfills a function in society.[1] Religious institutions are no exceptions. Religious institutions have many functions in society and while these functions may vary somewhat from society to society — contrast the role of religion in secular democracies such as the United States of America with its role in Islamic states such as Iran — they have many elements in common. One of the central functions of every religion is helping believers deal with suffering. No institution is as well equipped as religion to help individuals fill this need. The reason for this is clear: religion is the institution in society that offers a perspective that transcends this world. Therefore for the religious person a very effective way of coping with a this-world suffering is by employing an other-world perspective. Through religion we hope to find some ultimate order in what is apparent disorder.

But religions in addition to being central in coping with suffering can themselves *cause* suffering. When a this-world situation threatens our religious vision the result can be acute suffering. Religion cannot perform its role in helping us bring some order into disorder. Such intense suffering often demands rethinking religious convictions; it did for our university community. God did not protect us as we had presumed God would. Our religious vision was not able to integrate our suffering.

A word about the scope of human suffering. Suffering is part of the human condition; no one can escape it: to be human is to suffer! How can we get in touch with the varieties of human suffering, the suffering for which we seek religion's help? But it is difficult to find a schema that reflects the gamut of human suffering. One approach groups these perceived disorders according to their three sources: *natural, human,* and *societal. Natural* sources of suffering refer to disorders arising within the realm of nature such as physical liabilities, disease, aging, dying as well as earthquakes, hurricanes, tornadoes, floods, droughts, fires. *Human* sources of suffering refer to sufferings occasioned by human choices — our own or others — that effect the fulfillment of our needs and desires for physiological well-being, security, belonging, respect, self-actualization, meaning, ultimate value.[2] *Societal* sources of suffering refer to sufferings originating from our membership in our own society — wealth (haves and have-nots), race, class, sex, color — as well as to the relationship of our society to other societies, especially those relationships involving conflict.

The above schema though comprehensive is rather impersonal. A more helpful way to get in touch with suffering is by relating it to the three dimensions of our existence — *physical, psychological, spiritual.* I've found that my students tend to identify all suffering with physical suffering, overlooking their psychological and spiritual suffering. But perceived disorders arise at each level, and we all suffer to varying degrees at each level. There is no problem getting in touch with *physical* suffering. The physical pain of ill health is perhaps the most common experience at this level. Of course these sufferings, like sufferings at each level, vary in magnitude — from the common cold to terminal disease. But as long as we experience them as disorders, they qualify as sufferings.

The second level, the *psychological,* is more difficult to get in touch with. I say this because often we shield ourselves from it, denying our pain rather than facing it squarely and dealing with it. This suffering arises not from physical pain but from emotional pain. Emotional pain results whenever there is a gap between our desires and the reality of our lives. Relationships are a common source of this pain. Indeed our university community suffered acute pain from the loss of treasured relationships through the automobile accidents. But this pain arises from limitless sources; it is as all-pervasive as our anxieties: from personal concerns about health and career to universal concerns over human poverty and violence. Emotional pain also stems from unconscious sources, from anxieties buried deep within us manifesting themselves in irrational behaviors, such as compulsions, neuroses, psychoses. We are concerned primarily with conscious suffering.

Emotional pain is indeed an objective response to much reality; we ought to feel loneliness at the loss of a loved one and sadness at the violence in our world. However, certain insights from Buddhist philosophy have helped me and my students appreciate how much *additional* emotional pain we cause ourselves by our inability to face squarely and deal with the reality of our lives. Buddhist thought is immensely complex; we are dealing with it partially and simplistically. First the Buddha observed that suffering is inherent in the human life process: birth, disease, old age, death. Second the Buddha noted that we humans bring much suffering upon ourselves by our inability to accept this reality; we cling to desires that conflict with reality. These desires do not change reality, but they do increase our suffering. Third he advised that relief from suffering results from letting go of *excessive* desire — desires are *excessive* when they conflict with reality — eliminating the gap between reality and desire. Peace can then emerge even amidst suffering. The Buddha observed that to the degree we move along with the stream of life, we find peace; to the degree we fight against the stream of life, we cause ourselves additional suffering. From a Buddhist perspective the accidental deaths of our students are an example of suffering inherent in the human condition; also from their perspective our inability to accept our losses augmented our suffering. I have found that recalling this truth has frequently kept me from intensifying emotional pain though it does not eliminate it.

The third level, the *spiritual,* is perhaps the hardest to acknowledge and to define. But it can be the most acute level of suffering. We can describe spiritual suffering as the emotional pain experienced when the ultimate meaning of our lives is threatened because we feel abandoned by God — as our university community felt after the accidents. We can also describe spiritual suffering as the emotional pain experienced when we attempt to live our lives alienated from our deepest selves. This suffering may relate to sinfulness. Many of us have locked ourselves into a self-centered approach to life, whether consciously or unconsciously. We have oriented ourselves toward satisfying our own needs and disregarded the needs of others. In so doing we have forgotten the teachings of our religion, repressed our deepest inner voices (our consciences) and followed blindly the dictates of our culture. We have become alienated from our true selves, living with little inner peace and joy. Our pain is the result of living at odds with the deepest orientation of our being: our orientation toward loving and serving God and others. We are examples of Augustine's dictum: "You have made us, O Lord, for Yourself, and our hearts are restless until they rest in You."

Awareness of suffering at this spiritual level can be occasioned by a variety of circumstances — circumstances not necessarily related to sinfulness. It may arise in mid-life with a discovery that our life is relatively meaningless because we have oriented ourselves around values that are not ultimate. This is the pain most frequently identified with the mid-life crisis. It may arise from our struggle to move away from certain culturally defined roles and to move toward fuller realization of our unique personal identity; this usually demands being true to our own inner voices rather than simply responding to societal expectations. In our society many women have witnessed to the pain of this struggle because they have been forced to fulfill societal expectations. Or it may arise as we attempt to respond to life's tragedies and find that our religious assumptions have been threatened — as it did for our university community. The accidents forced us to examine our basic beliefs in a God who loves and cares for us.

Spiritual suffering is rampant in contemporary society. For those of us whose spiritual dimension is centered in God, this pain involves our relationship to God. And acknowledging this pain can be the occasion for reorienting our lives to God. Often it is the intensity of our physical and emotional pain that leads to this reorientation.

I know of nothing in modern fiction that better illustrates spiritual suffering — as well as physical and psychological suffering — than "The Death of Ivan Ilyich" by Tolstoy.[3] Ivan Ilyich is a successful, middle-aged Russian magistrate. All his life Ivan has accepted and followed unquestioningly his society's guidelines for success and happiness. But now Ivan is dying from an accidental injury contracted four months previously. His physical condition has progressively deteriorated; Ivan has been unable to face his situation. It is three days before his death. Gerazim is his servant.

> The doctor said his physical agony was dreadful, and that was true; but even more dreadful was his moral agony, and it was this that tormented him most.
>
> What had induced his moral agony was that during the night, as he gazed at Gerazim's broad-boned, sleepy, good-natured face, he suddenly asked himself: "What if my entire life, my entire conscious life, simply was *not the real thing*?"
>
> It occurred to him that what had seemed utterly inconceivable before — that he had not lived the kind of life he should have — might in fact be true. It occurred to him that those scarcely perceptible impulses of his to protest what people of high rank considered good, vague impulses which he had always suppressed, might have been precisely what mattered, and all the rest not been the real thing. . . .
>
> . . . When, in the morning, he saw first the footman, then his wife, then his daughter, and then the doctor, their every gesture, their every word, confirmed the horrible truth revealed to him during the night. In them he saw himself, all he had lived by, saw clearly that all this was not the real thing but a dreadful, enormous deception that shut out both life and death. This awareness intensified his physical sufferings, magnified them tenfold.[4]

In a book proposing to deal with suffering from a religious perspective it is important to reiterate that human suffering typically involves more than physical suffering. Most intense human suffering involves all three levels. Persons with terminal illness — like Ivan Ilyich — experience physical suffering from their disease, but simultaneously even more intense psychological suffering over the effect of their disease on their loved ones and spiritual suffering over the meaningfulness of their prior life and their own survival after death. And religion is central for two reasons: first, it is often the only effective way of dealing with suffering; second, as we have said, if inadequate it can contribute to the intensity of suffering. Our university community suffered intensely both from the psychological pain of lost friendships and from spiritual anxiety from the threat to our religious vision — it seemed as though God had abandoned us.

Just as suffering originates from the three dimensions of our being, so it can be dealt with at these same three dimensions: physiological, psychological, spiritual. Our specific concern is the role of religion in handling suffering. Commonly we deal with suffering solely on the first two levels; we take medicine for illness and resign ourselves psychologically to life's inevitable disappointments. Rarely do we deal with suffering on the religious level — and only when forced to because the physical and psychological are insufficient. This is unfortunate. We who believe in God believe that God has a role in all of life, and therefore a role in handling suffering. For religious persons handling suffering effectively demands finding a way of transforming the perceived disorders of life — at whatever level — into some kind of perceived order consistent with religious beliefs and actually enriching our relationship with God.

Though the religious dimension can be important in handling every suffering, it is often the crucial dimension in successfully handling acute suffering. I am continually moved by the conclusion of "The Death of Ivan Ilyich." It is now the hour before Ivan's death.

> "Yes, all of it was simply *not the real thing*. But no matter. I can still make it *the real thing* — I can. But what *is* the real thing?" Ivan Ilyich asked himself and suddenly grew quiet.
>
> . . . Just then he felt someone kissing his hand. He opened his eyes and looked at his son. He grieved for him. His wife came in and went up to him. He looked at her. She gazed at him with an open mouth, with unwiped tears on her nose and cheeks, with a look of despair on her face. He grieved for her.
>
> "Yes, I'm torturing them," he thought. "They feel sorry for me, but it will be better for them when I die." He wanted to tell them this but lacked the strength to speak. "But why speak — I must do something," he thought. He looked at his wife and, indicating his son with a glance, said:
>
> "Take him away . . . sorry for him . . . and you." He wanted to add: "Forgive" but instead said "Forget," and too feeble to correct himself, dismissed it, knowing that He who needed to understand would understand.

... "How good and how simple!" he thought. "And the pain?" he asked himself. "Where has it gone? Now, then, pain, where are you?"[5]

Only in the moments before his death did Ivan break the bonds of his self-centeredness and reach out for forgiveness. Only in these moments did he reach the religious level of response to his suffering — and find peace.

I am moved also by the reflections of the Jewish psychiatrist Viktor Frankl on his internment in Nazi concentration camps. Frankl concludes that only those who could find meaning for life survived: those with a *why* could survive any *how.* He noted that if his fellow inmates' ultimate beliefs and values held up, they survived; if they did not, they gave up the will to live and eventually died.

> As we said before, any attempt to restore a man's inner strength in the camp had first to succeed in showing him some future goal. Nietzsche's words, "He who has a *why* to live for can bear with almost any how," could be the guiding motto for all psychotherapeutic and psychohygienic efforts regarding prisoners. Whenever there was an opportunity for it, one had to give them a why, an aim for their lives in order to strengthen them to bear the terrible *how* of their existence. Woe to him who saw no more sense in his life, no aim, no purpose, and therefore no point in carrying on. He was soon lost. The typical reply with which such a man rejected all encouraging arguments was, "I have nothing to expect from life any more."[6]

If the spiritual dimension of our lives holds together in suffering, we can face all that life may bring. For believers religion provides this spiritual dimension and gives the ultimate why.

At our university many of our students were experiencing the greatest suffering of their lives; it became necessary to find new reserves of strength to cope with it effectively. Most had dealt with previous sufferings only on the physiological and psychological levels. For the first time many were turning to faith as a means of dealing with suffering. But the tragedies challenged their faith. Before their faith could strengthen them, they needed to know that their ultimate beliefs about a loving God could hold up, even in light of the recent tragedies. The *why* for their living needed to be deepened in order to cope with the *how* of untimely deaths of friends. Frequently suffering becomes the key that opens the spiritual dimension. And it is never too late, as we've seen with Ivan Ilyich.

## Religion: Meaning Context and Support Context

In my observation when we religiously oriented people do decide to use our beliefs to deal with suffering we spontaneously do so in two distinctive ways. These two ways relate directly to our assumptions about God's relationship to this world, and, therefore, to how we expect God to act to help us in our suffering. These spontaneous reactions involve different assumptions about the help we can receive from God in suffering, assumptions rarely reflected upon and even more rarely articulated. Throughout this book I will refer to these two mindsets for approaching God in suffering by two terms: the *meaning context approach* and the *support context approach.* This unusual terminology is my own and I am using it simply to refer to the two typical ways of dealing with suffering used by religiously oriented people. In my experience we all use both ways but we do tend to focus more energy on one or the other approach. It is the thesis of this book that — at least for Christians — the meaning context approach always remains inadequate and must always be supplemented by the support context approach.

We begin with the *meaning context approach.* The religious person striving to make sense of suffering within the meaning context seeks to understand why God sent the suffering, asking the question "Why, O God?" Persons dealing with suffering using the meaning context have two specific assumptions about God's relationship to the world and to suffering: **1) God is the direct cause of suffering; 2) God causes suffering for a specific reason.** Since the reason for suffering is known by God, we ask to see our suffering through God's perspective. We assume that if we knew God's reason for sending the suffering, acceptance of it would be easier. In the meaning context approach what we perceive initially as disordered and threatening to our religious vision can through faith become ordered and integrated within this vision, *if* we know God's reasons. The most pious among us may even acknowledge that God knows best — even though God's ways are not our ways. Others, however, may simply rage against God's ways — no matter what God's reasons. Most of us begin our attempts to cope with suffering within the meaning context. Our university community did.

The insights of Dr. Elisabeth Kübler-Ross reveal the pervasiveness of the meaning context approach for religiously oriented people.[7] Through her interviews with dying patients she noted a fivefold process in dealing with terminal illness: *Denial, Anger, Bargaining, Depression, Acceptance.* Her observations regarding the process of dealing with death apply to those who believe in God as well as to those who don't; my observations assume belief in God. Each of the stages reflects an approach to God typical of the meaning context mindset. I believe her conclusions are apt for dealing not only with terminal illness but also with all significant suffering.

The first stage, *Denial,* reinforces the observation that most of us choose to deal with suffering by denying its existence or minimizing its magnitude — the Buddha is right! We tell ourselves that we are not suffering or that it is not so bad and will go away soon, so let's just get on with our lives.[8] Denial may be helpful in the initial stages of coping with suffering until we can muster the resources to face it squarely. However, it is not a successful way to cope in the long run since we must continue to use much psychic energy to deny an obvious fact.

The second stage is *Anger.* When the fact of suffering must be faced because the psychological efforts at denial are failing, the question arises, "Why me?" Having admitted the reality of the suffering, we are now angry that our life has been so threatened. And typically this anger does not remain within us; it is projected onto others, often to those most close, to family members, friends, doctors and nurses. And onto God. If we have a religious orientation the question becomes, "Why me, O God?" Hasn't God willed and caused the suffering? If God caused it, can't God also take it away? In Kübler-Ross' observations the initial use of the meaning context involves anger at God. Ivan is a good example. After two months of denial he is finally forced to face the reality of his increased pain and loss of health. For the first time he breaks down.

> He cried about his helplessness, about his terrible loneliness, about the cruelty of people, about the cruelty of God, about the absence of God.
>
> "Why hast Thou done all this? Why hast Thou brought me to this? Why doest Thou torture me so? For what?"
>
> He did not expect an answer, and he cried because there was no answer and there could be none. The pain started up again, but he

did not stir, did not call out. He said to himself: "Go on then! Hit me again! But what for? What for? What have I done to Thee?"[9]

And after Denial and Anger comes the third stage: *Bargaining.* We begin bargaining with God for the removal of our suffering, promising anything should God deign to mitigate or take away our suffering or at least extend our life. But the bargaining is fruitless. We are forced by facts to face both the reality and the magnitude of our suffering. We enter the fourth stage: *Depression.* Our suffering is real; it will not be taken away or even mitigated by God. We are depressed. In this stage we may find our faith threatened to the core. We have always been firm believers in God. But no response has been given by God to our pleas. When we need God most God is absent. What's the use of faith? Where is God? For Christians Christ's words on the cross express it well, "My God, my God, why have You forsaken me?"

The fifth state, *Acceptance,* comes only at the end of the process of grieving. In Kübler-Ross' observations Acceptance means resignation; it should not be mistaken for a happy stage: "It is almost void of feelings. It is as if the pain had gone, the struggle is over, and there comes a time for 'the final rest before the long journey.'"[10] But religious people may move beyond this resignation and toward a surrender to God's will and an increased confidence in God. This confidence may be accompanied by deep peace and even joy — as it was for Ivan Ilyich in his final moments. What had been initially perceived as a very threatening disorder on a this-worldly level is now perceived as ordered through the other-worldly perspective of faith. This stage, however, seems to emerge only after suffering through the intervening stages of Bargaining and Depression. Arriving at this final stage too easily may indicate that we have not allowed ourselves to experience the full impact of the suffering. It should be noted the stages reoccur and that their order may vary.

How do we expect God to help us in our suffering? Within the meaning context the answer is simple: by taking it away or mitigating it. Implicit in the meaning context approach is a belief that God is in direct control of all the external events of creation and history, and therefore God should be able to control the events of our life. But if God will not take suffering away or mitigate it — impossible if it has occurred — then we ask God to reveal the reasons for sending it. Our assumption is simple: God's wisdom and power are infinite. If we knew

God's reasons we could more readily perceive our suffering not as disordered but as ordered, as integral to God's plan.

An important clarification must be made. In claiming that the meaning context approach to suffering is ultimately insufficient I am not implying that suffering has no meaning. Just the opposite. The remainder of this book seeks to present a Christian approach to suffering which views human suffering as a meaningful factor in human existence — perhaps the most meaningful factor in defining the kind of person and the kind of Christian we ultimately become. It surely was for Ivan Ilyich. In rejecting the meaning context approach as inadequate I am rejecting simply the mindset that holds 1) that God is the *direct cause* of suffering and 2) that God causes every suffering for a *specific reason*. The attempts to see God as the direct cause of suffering and project reasons onto God have led many to great frustration and even to a rejection of God. God's relationship to the world's suffering remains ultimately mysterious. For most of us, therefore, the meaning context approach is not an effective way to transform perceived disorders into a perceived order. It surely wasn't for our university community. Nor for Ivan Ilyich. Fortunately there is another way.

The religious person striving to cope with suffering also approaches God in a second way — through the *support context approach.* The cry to God is not "Why, O God?" but rather "Help me, O God!" Persons dealing with suffering using the support context also have specific assumptions about God's relationship to the world and to suffering: **1) God gives strength for life; 2) God gives strength in suffering.** In the support context mindset our primary focus is on God the source of strength to deal with suffering and not on God the cause of our suffering. The meaning question may remain, but it's in the background.

In the support context mindset the foundation of faith is an experienced relationship with God. Since we ground belief on experience, we are less dependent upon external events for maintaining it. While ever acknowledging God as the creator and sustainer of the universe, we also accept our inability to grasp God's ways. The resolution of suffering comes from the conviction — and often even the experience — that God is with us. Since we are able to experience our relationship with God even during suffering, the ultimate beliefs and values of our life remain intact; the world remains ordered. What we perceive initially as disordered and threatening to our faith vision can now be integrated within this vision knowing that God will give sufficient strength — even though the disorder remains. Significantly, the resolution of Ivan Ilyich's suffering occurred not through intellectual answers to his questions but through a heightened experience of God. Therefore the support context approach becomes the most reliable way of transforming perceived disorders into a perceived order. No matter what happens God remains with us and so the foundations of our lives remain intact!

Where is God in suffering? The two mindsets described have distinctive approaches to God for coping with suffering. The meaning context approach seeks evidence of God primarily in external events of creation and history. It seeks to resolve suffering by asking God to remove or mitigate suffering — or at the least reveal reasons for it. The support context approach seeks evidence of God in the experience of the relationship with God. It seeks to resolve suffering through an enhanced experience of this relationship, one equal to the need. For most religious people, these two mindsets coexist and are used in greater or lesser degree in dealing with suffering. The goal for religiously oriented persons is a transformation of experience from faith-threatening to faith-integrated. The following diagram illustrates the schema I have presented in this chapter for dealing with suffering within a religious perspective.

## Diagram 1
### Two Religious Approaches to Suffering

**Meaning Context:
Why, O God?**

1. God is the direct cause of suffering
2. God causes suffering for a specific reason

**Support Context:
Help me, O God!**

1. God gives strength for life
2. God gives strength in suffering

Perceived Disorder: Faith-Threatening

Perceived Order: Faith-Integrated

In my many years at our university I had never observed God's presence so palpably among us as during the aftermath of the accidents — supporting us individually, drawing us into community, giving us the resources to strengthen one another, especially to support the family members of the deceased students. Many students commented to me that without this strength they didn't know how they could handle their suffering. Yet we continued to ask where God was. We undervalued the personal strength we were receiving from our relationship to God and focused on seeking God's reasons for "taking" our friends. And our conclusions left us unsatisfied. From my point of view they insulted God by not acknowledging either God's presence throughout the experience or God's gift of freedom given to us to direct our own lives.

I believe our community — including myself — had a great need to clarify our assumptions about how we expected God to act in our lives. Our failure to do this was intensifying our suffering. At a time when we needed God most there was a part of us that continued to hold God at a distance. I eventually came to see that some of our confusion could be traced to Scripture itself. I believe that the Old Testament has a distinctively different focus in dealing with suffering than the New Testament. It seems to me that we Christians have not adequately appreciated the New Testament revelation and are still approaching life and suffering basically from an Old Testament perspective.

## Where Is Our God?

How is God revealed in this world? Both Old and New Testaments[11] share similar beliefs: God is revealed in creation, in history, and within human experience. God is the God of creation: the visible beauty of creation reflects the invisible beauty of its Creator. God is the God of history: the history of the world is salvation history and God works within history to bring the world to its final culmination in Christ. And God dwells within us: God's presence gives wisdom and strength. We can draw many conclusions about God that are true for both Jewish and Christian traditions.

In both Old and New Testaments God is the God of history and of creation; therefore both traditions are similar in presenting God as the *ultimate meaning context* of all reality — as the familiar spiritual puts it, "He's got the whole world in his hands." Further since in both Old and New Testaments God is also presented as dwelling within and relating personally to the human community, it is true to say that both traditions are similar in presenting God as the *ultimate support context* — God is shepherd, redeemer, father, friend. For Christians and Jews God is the ultimate source of meaning in life as well as the ultimate source of strength.

But these assertions must be nuanced when dealing with how the Old and New Testaments approach suffering. It is not sufficient to assert similarity. It is my contention that the Old Testament presents a different approach to understanding and coping with suffering than the New Testament. Though both approaches are present in each Testament, the meaning context approach dominates the Old Testament while the support context approach dominates the New Testament. Each Testament is influenced by its basic focus on how God works in the world.

While never denying God's manifestation interiorly within the person, the Old Testament focuses on a God of history and creation. The Exodus from Egypt and the revelation to Moses on Mount Sinai are the heart of God's manifestation. The devout Jew inspired by the Hebrew Scriptures therefore seeks to make sense of suffering by looking at historical events and asking for reasons for God's actions in light of the Exodus-Sinai events. The dominant Jewish tradition — a tradition challenged by the Book of Job — lends itself to using a meaning context approach in dealing with suffering. The primary prayer becomes, "Why are You doing this to me, O God?" Rabbi Harold Kushner's best seller *When Bad Things Happen to Good People*[12] situates itself squarely within this orientation though ultimately challenging it.

In contrast the New Testament, while never ignoring the role of God in history and creation, focuses on God who works primarily within the person through Jesus and the Holy Spirit. The heart of Christian revelation is the paschal mystery which culminates in the sending of the Holy Spirit at Pentecost thereby continuing Jesus' presence to believers. This revelation lends itself to the use of a support context approach in dealing with suffering. The devout Christian inspired by the New Testament therefore sees God's primary manifestation since Jesus' resurrection occurring through the work of the Holy Spirit sent by Jesus and the Father. The Christian praying within this mindset seeks strength in suffering through a personal faith relationship praying not "Why are You doing this to me, O God?" but "Help me, O Lord!"

This book develops these basic insights. Chapter II focuses upon the role of the Holy Spirit in Christian life using insights from the New Testament. Chapter III examines the Old Testament message concerning God as the rewarder of the just and punisher of the evil as well as the challenge to this message presented by the Book of Job. Chapter IV returns to the New Testament examining Jesus and Paul first for the role of the Holy Spirit in their lives and then for their approach to suffering. Chapter V examines the role of Jesus in the lives of Christians and draws out the implications of this role for dealing with suffering. Chapter VI concludes with a reflection from a Christian perspective on the possibility of reconciling an all-powerful and all-loving God with the existence of so much evil and suffering in this world. Whereas Chapters II to V flow directly from reflection on Scripture, Chapter VI is highly tentative and speculative — reconciling a God of love with evil and suffering will always remain one of life's deepest mysteries.

It is important to point out the limited scope of this book. First, it is pastoral. It is intended to be a practical help for Christians in using faith more effectively to deal with suffering. It was originally prompted by the observation that my university community suffered even more intensely because of our failure to grasp the Christian message on suffering. My explanations, therefore, attempt to avoid overly technical scriptural exegesis and theological speculations.

Second, it is concerned with individual suffering rather than with societal suffering. I am aware that I have not adequately addressed the horrendous sufferings of our time arising within the social context. My life experience makes it suitable for me to limit my scope, leaving social problems to others with greater experience. However, the goal of my book is to present an approach to suffering flowing from Jesus' message on the Kingdom of God and so containing implications for social justice.

Please note that in keeping with the pastoral and personal focus of the book I have included reflection questions at the end of each chapter. The questions are intended to help the reader apply ideas from the text to personal experiences. To get the most from the book I suggest a three-fold process of reading the text, answering the reflection questions individually, and finally sharing responses with others. The book will be most helpful to those readers who get beyond the discussion of ideas and take the time to react to the text in light of their own personal experiences. It is ideal for small discussion groups — providing the groups enjoy a significant trust level.

No one is an expert in understanding and dealing with suffering. Each of us has unique insights and experiences — though we frequently do not explicate them since the social context for such sharing is usually lacking. This book will achieve its purpose if it stimulates greater awareness of our habitual ways of dealing with suffering and brings these ways into dialogue with the New Testament message.

## A Personal Note

Some information about my background will be helpful in putting this book into its proper context. I have mentioned that the desire to write this book occurred initially at the time of the auto accidents. But the development of insights for the book began long before this occurrence. My primary interest in theology has always been spirituality. My doctoral dissertation compares Thomas Merton and Abraham Maslow in their approaches to religious experience. After graduate school I focused on the role of the Holy Spirit in Christian life. I have used my insights on the Holy Spirit to develop many of my courses: prayer, discernment, mysticism, sin and grace, religion and personality. Also I have used these insights on the Spirit as the focus of my two previous books, as their titles suggest: *In His Spirit: A Guide to Today's Spirituality,* an introduction to the spiritual life with a focus on personal prayer, and *Moving in the Spirit: Becoming a Contemplative in Action,* a practical approach to finding God in daily life inspired by St. Ignatius Loyola's Rules for Discernment of Spirits as found in his *Spiritual Exercises.*[13] And the Spirit remains the focus of this book, as its title implies: *Finding God in Troubled Times: The Holy Spirit and Suffering.*

I am a college teacher. About the time of the accidents I began teaching a course on suffering: Understanding and Dealing with Suffering: Buddhist, Hebrew and Christian Perspectives. The purpose of the course was — and is — to compare these traditions for their theoretical as well as practical approaches to suffering. The Christian tradition was, indeed, one of the traditions, but I taught this course for several years with no reference to the Holy Spirit. Comparatively recently I was struck by the centrality of the Holy Spirit for dealing with suffering. I have revised the course to reflect this focus.

I ask myself why it took me so long to formally integrate insights on the Holy Spirit with my approach to suffering. I am not sure of the answer. I suspect it flows from a very human tendency to deny the reality of much of my own suffering. My previous work has focused on the richness of human life when transformed by the Holy Spirit; it has not focused upon the role of the Spirit in dealing with life's trials. I suspect also that I needed the benefit of years to face with equanimity certain aspects of my own life. My current age, fifty-something, has given me that benefit! Perhaps also recent personal sufferings demanded deeper integration with faith. But I suspect I am not untypical in permitting suffering to be one of the last aspects of life to be integrated more consciously with living the Gospel.

Authors work out insights within specific religious traditions. Mine is the Roman Catholic tradition. I have been delightfully surprised, however, that many Protestant friends, lay and ordained, have found my previous books helpful. Within the past two years I have accepted invitations and presented workshops based on my books to Christians from six differing Protestant traditions. I count it a great blessing that my work is the occasion for the Spirit to unite the Church of Christ so broadly. May this book be similarly blessed!

Finally, I am an extrovert. My classroom is the laboratory for working out my insights. From the classroom insights eventually find their way into print. So with this book. Frequently I refer to classroom dialogues in subsequent chapters. It is the candid reactions of my students that have forced me to be clear. Likewise it is their openness and trust, both in and beyond the classroom, that have forced me to be real. They made me abandon clichés that didn't speak to their real life sufferings. This book is dedicated to my students. Many of their faces remain vividly before me as I write.

Is it presumptuous for someone to write on suffering whose life has been largely devoid of major sufferings? Perhaps. Yet suffering is part of the human condition, of my life, of every life. Sooner or later we are invited by God to face it squarely. And then we may have a comforting word for one another, limited though it may be. I share the sentiments of Daniel Simundson, a fellow-author of a book on suffering.

*My* truth about the meaning of suffering is not ultimate truth — it is earthly, contextual, pragmatic, trying to bring some comfort. If a specific explanation for suffering helps someone to endure that suffering, it is certainly useful. If it does not help them, it should be discarded. At the very least, we need to think about questions like this, with all the brainpower God has given us, in order to sort out those answers that are less helpful, or even harmful to a continuing faith.[14]

Only in this spirit do I have the courage to offer *Finding God in Troubled Times: The Holy Spirit and Suffering.*

## REFLECTION QUESTIONS

1. Do you recognize the five stages presented by Kübler-Ross as describing how you usually deal with suffering? Explain. Give examples.

2. Recall the major sufferings of your *past life.* Was your faith helpful in dealing with them? Explain.

3. To what extent did you use the meaning context mindset to handle these sufferings? Did God give you reasons for causing the sufferings? Explain. Do you believe God is the direct cause of the world's sufferings? Explain.

4. To what extent did you use the support context mindset? Did God give you strength? Explain. In general, do you experience strength when you go to God in your sufferings? Explain.

5. What are the major sufferings of your *present life*? Do you use your faith to deal with them? Do you use the meaning context or the support context approach? Explain.

# II. HOW DOES GOD WORK IN THE WORLD?

How does God work in our world? All Christians assent to the first article of the Apostles' Creed: "I believe in God the Father Almighty, creator of heaven and earth." The article asserts that the world proceeds from God initially, is sustained in existence by God now, and will remain in existence as long as God determines. This truth is a foundation of Christian faith.

But there is a further dimension to the question. In addition to creating and sustaining the world in existence, how does God act in our daily lives? Though the question is simple, its answer, emphatically, is not. Among Christians there is a wide variety of beliefs, beliefs strongly held and often at variance with one another. To get in touch with our personal beliefs, it is helpful to ask ourselves the following question: "How does God act in our daily lives?" I've found that the most effective way to open my course on suffering is to write this question on the board and then to ask the students to discuss their own assumptions. Most of them have never explicitly reflected on this question and so are initially stymied by it. Gradually opinions are tentatively put forth. Their response to this question uncovers their habitual assumptions. Before dealing explicitly with God's relationship to suffering, it is important to clarify our general assumptions about how God acts in the world.

I believe there are four possible responses to this question about God's activity in our daily lives.[1] **First, God works in the world in human hearts through the transforming power of the Holy Spirit.** Clearly the New Testament puts primary emphasis on this dimension. The Father and Jesus send the Spirit to take Jesus' place after the Resurrection. The Christian life now is a life in response to the Spirit working in human hearts. Love is the primary effect of God's action in human life.

**Second, in addition to working in human hearts God also works within the laws of nature** *though in a hidden way.* The question is whether God intervenes within these laws of nature. This position maintains that God does indeed intervene within these laws but as their author God continues to respect them and work within them in a hidden way. For instance, should a person be healed physically in response to prayer we can assert that God has intervened by influencing the recuperative processes of the body. Though God does intervene, it is impossible to claim that the intervention is a miracle because the intervention could be understood as an aspect of natural law not fully understood.

**Third, in addition to working within human hearts and within the laws of nature in a hidden way, God also intervenes in creation and works** *contrary to* **the laws of nature.** This position states that God as the author of the world freely intervenes in the physical universe *in a miraculous way,* even contradicting its normal operations. Some have witnessed and testified to physical healings totally unexplainable and contradictory to physical laws; others have witnessed and testified to obvious interruptions of the physical laws of the universe, such as the sun spinning in the heaven at Fatima. These types of divine intervention are called miracles.

**Finally, God works in all of the above ways.** God works within human hearts by the transforming action of the Holy Spirit and God also works in creation and history both in hidden as well as in miraculous ways. This position admits variations. We could assert, for instance, that God works in all the above ways but most rarely in the miraculous way.

Perhaps an even more pointed question to ask ourselves is how we *expect* God to act in our lives now. The question is crucial because it forces us to articulate how we understand God's role in causing and taking away suffering. Do we expect God to intervene in the natural order either to prevent or to mitigate suffering? It was clear to me that many of our students expected God to prevent the tragic accidents that occurred at our university. This assumption implied that they expected God either to control the faculties of the drunken drivers, thus preventing the accidents from occurring in the first place; or to intervene in the operation of the laws of nature by not permitting them to run their course, for instance, by preventing the second car from rolling down the embankment and thereby killing our students.

It is difficult to uncover our implicit assumptions. A helpful way is to look at our prayers of petition and thanksgiving. What do we pray for? What do we thank God for? What do these prayers imply about our views on God's action in our world?

How does God work in the world? We all agree that created reality proceeds from God, is sustained in existence by God and one day at the end of time will be drawn back into God with Christ as its center — the Alpha and Omega of all creation. In this sense God is continually working in creation and history. In addition to this, how do we *expect* God to work in our lives now? Our belief has implications for using Christian faith to deal with suffering and relates directly to the two approaches to dealing with suffering described in Chapter I. The meaning context mindset expects that God normally intervenes in the laws of nature either by causing suffering or by removing or mitigating it; the support context mindset expects that God works within the human heart giving strength to deal with suffering but does not expect God to alter the laws of nature. There is no consensus among Christians.

My personal belief, however, is that God works in our lives primarily through the Spirit in human hearts. In asserting this I intend to honor the revelation of the New Testament about the Father's sending the Spirit to take the place of Jesus. My reflections will focus on what we can expect God to do in light of the presence of the Holy Spirit in our hearts. Since this is my belief, I approach God within the support context mindset, seeking strength from the Holy Spirit to cope with suffering lovingly and creatively; I do not approach God within the meaning context mindset. I am uncomfortable with the implications of the meaning context because it expects that God works in the world normally by intervening in the operation of the physical laws of nature; it expects God to prevent, to cause or to take suffering away. To me the extent of human suffering makes this unlikely. I do not, however, deny that God may work in these other ways.

By examining the New Testament message on the Holy Spirit we are establishing the context for understanding all Christian spirituality. We will apply this understanding in subsequent chapters to understanding the role of the Holy Spirit in dealing with suffering. We begin by describing two models of the self with reference to the role of the Holy Spirit — the Scriptural Model and the Capitalistic Model.[2] We conclude with a description of Christian spirituality in light of the Spirit's role.

### Scriptural Model: Self-in-God

What is the role of the Holy Spirit in Christian spirituality? In a recent encyclical letter Pope John Paul II expressed succinctly the centrality of the Holy Spirit in Christian life. Italics are in original text.

> The *Redemption accomplished by the Son* in the dimensions of the earthly history of humanity — accomplished in his "departure" through the Cross and Resurrection — is at the same time, in its entire salvific power, *transmitted to the Holy Spirit:* the one who "will take what is mine." The words of the text of John indicate that, according to the divine plan, Christ's "departure" is an indispensable condition for the "sending" and the coming of the Holy Spirit, but these words also say that what begins now is *the new salvific self-giving of God, in the Holy Spirit.*[3]

The phrase "in its entire salvific power" is key. The pope is teaching that absolutely nothing occurs as the result of the redemption of the Son outside the action of the Holy Spirit. In so teaching the pope is simply reasserting the age-old tradition that the Holy Spirit is our sanctifier: the Father creates, the Son redeems, the Spirit sanctifies. The Spirit is the principle of our sanctification.

It is significant that in the very next paragraph the pope reaffirms another Christian tradition: the Spirit is the principle of our existence, and of the existence of all creation. The Book of Genesis describes the creation as a work of the Spirit of God. But in affirming this truth, the pope wants to distinguish this work of the Spirit *before* from the work of the Spirit *after* the resurrection of Jesus. The sending of the Spirit by the Father and Jesus after the resurrection initiates a new creation, a new beginning. The pope continues:

> It is a *new beginning* in relation to the first, original beginning of God's salvific self-giving, which is identified with the mystery of creation itself. Here is what we read in the very first words of the Book of Genesis: "In the beginning God created the heavens and the earth

> . . . and the Spirit of God (*ruah Elohim*) *was moving over the face of the waters.*" This biblical concept of creation includes not only the call to existence of the very being of the cosmos, that is to say *the giving of existence,* but also the presence of the Spirit of God in creation, that is to say the beginning of God's salvific self-communication to the things he creates. This is true *first of all concerning man,* who has been created in the image and likeness of God: "Let us make man in our image, after our likeness."[4]

The pope presents the Spirit as the energizing factor of all creation, human and non-human. But this new beginning — this new infusion of the Spirit — has as a condition the departure of Jesus. The encyclical cites Jesus' promise to his disciples at the last supper, "But I tell you the truth, it is better for you that I go. For if I do not go, the Advocate will not come to you. But if I go, I will send him to you" (Jn 16:7).[5] Pentecost is the Christian feast celebrating this coming of the Holy Spirit to the first Christian community. The encyclical focuses upon the implications of this new presence of the Holy Spirit for Christian living.

In the decades since Vatican Council II Christians, especially Catholics, have been recovering their awareness of the role of the Spirit in Christian life. The Catholic tradition spearheaded by the Council of Trent in the sixteenth century and Vatican Council I in the nineteenth century had encouraged Catholics to guide their lives by fidelity to the teaching of the institutional Church. Little attention was given to the role of the Spirit in Christian life. For Catholic Christians Vatican II has corrected that imbalance.

This omission had great effect on the understanding of most Christians — Catholics especially — on how God works in the world. Since we had no real awareness of the role of the Spirit in our lives, we did not understand this as a primary way God worked. We were, however, convinced that God was active in the world. Without giving the matter too much thought we more or less presumed that God's activity is focused primarily in creation and history outside ourselves, and so we looked to it for evidences of God's work. I believe this was true for my university community when we began questioning God's role after the automobile deaths of our students.

To appreciate more fully the role of the Spirit in our lives it is helpful to contrast two views of the self focusing on the relationship between

God and self: the Scriptural Model (the Self-in-God model) and the Capitalistic Model (the Self-outside-God model). The following diagram is helpful. The Scriptural Model respects the centrality of the Spirit within the self for all good actions; the Capitalistic Model disregards entirely the role of the Spirit.[6] Note that in the diagram I am using the word *God* for *Spirit*. The New Testament clearly attributes God's presence among us after the Resurrection to the Holy Spirit. I could also use the word *Jesus,* since the New Testament frequently identifies the presence of the Spirit with the presence of Jesus. The triangles are helpful for contrasting the two models for the presence and absence of the Spirit. The concentric circles, however, are crucial for highlighting the interaction of the Spirit with the three dimensions of the self: body, mind and spirit — *body* and *mind* refer to our physiological and psychological dimensions and *spirit* refers to our freedom, our capacity to respond to or to resist God's movements.

In the Scriptural Model the triangles representing God and the self clearly overlap, indicating that the activity of God occurs within the self and that God is ultimately the source of all good actions. Several key insights taken from the New Testament should be highlighted. **First, God is present in the self.** In the New Testament the primary presence of God is within the believing community. Paul's letters reflect this truth in two especially powerful images. Referring to the Christian community he unambiguously asserts that they are the Body of Christ (1 Cor 12:12) and the temples of the Holy Spirit (1 Cor 3:16–17). This indwelling of the Spirit in our hearts has traditionally been referred to as sanctifying grace. The Gospels assert this same truth of Jesus' presence in human beings in various ways. For me the most striking illustration of this truth is Matthew's Last Judgment scene in Chapter 25. It is the end of the world; the Son of Man (usually identified with Jesus) has returned and is judging humans on a very simple criterion — love for one another: I was hungry and you gave me to eat, thirsty and you gave me to drink. And those being judged are confused and ask when they did such good deeds, not recognizing themselves as having given food and drink to Jesus. And the Son of Man (Jesus) asserts simply, "Amen, I say to you, whatever you did for one of these brothers of mine, you did for me" (Mt 25:40). Note the contrast with the Western Model — God is totally outside the self.

## Diagram 2
## Source of Good Actions:
## Relationship between God and Self

**Scriptural Model:**
**Self-in-God**

**Capitalistic Model:**
**Self-outside-God**

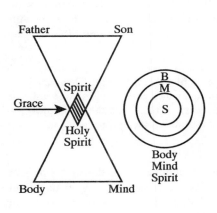

**God initiates;**
**Self responds.**

**God:** Present
Acting
Initiating
Transforming

**Self:** Responding
Not responding

**Self initiates;**
**God rewards.**

**God:** Rewarding
Not rewarding

**Self:** Initiating
Not initiating

**Second, God is active in the self.** Recall that the concentric circles highlight the interaction of the Holy Spirit with the three dimensions of the self — body, mind, spirit. God's presence in us is dynamic. The most dramatic illustration of this truth is the account of the coming of the Spirit to the first Christian community at Pentecost in the Acts of the Apostles. Jesus appeared to his disciples gathered in Jerusalem, telling them to remain in Jerusalem and to await the coming of the Spirit. They inquired whether at this time the kingdom would be restored. He responded it was not for them to know the Father's plans but promised them that they would receive power when the Holy Spirit comes and then be his witnesses in Jerusalem, Judea, Samaria and all the ends of the earth. And indeed at Pentecost the Spirit did descend on this community.

> And suddenly there came from the sky a noise like a strong driving wind, and it filled the entire house in which they were. Then there appeared to them tongues as of fire, which parted and came to rest on each one of them. And they were all filled with the holy Spirit and began to speak in different tongues, as the Spirit enabled them to proclaim (Acts 2:2–4).

The disciples — who had virtually abandoned Jesus during his passion and were hiding in the upper room for fear of the Jews — were then filled with faith and began witnessing to Jesus; most were eventually martyred for their faith. The entire Acts of the Apostles chronicles the activity of the disciples under the inspiration of the Holy Spirit. Again note the contrast with the Capitalistic Model; since God is not present in the self, God can have no effect on motivation or action.

**Third, God initiates all good desires and actions within the self.** So intimate and all-pervasive is this presence and action of the Spirit in the human heart that the Church relying on the New Testament teaches that there is no movement toward good in human beings apart from the action of the Spirit. Traditionally we have called this action of God actual grace. This truth was disputed in the fourth and fifth centuries by groups called today Pelagians and Semi-Pelagians. These groups claimed that after baptism the only grace needed for certain good deeds was the external teaching and example of Jesus. Christians were called upon to live lives in conformity with this teaching and example by using all their natural powers. The role of the internal power of the Spirit was under-valued. Augustine reasserted the New Testament teaching on grace. The internal power of the Spirit is central to all good deeds. Indeed the very first desire for good comes from God within the self — not from the self apart from God. We wouldn't even have these desires if God were not present. The Christian is called to respond always to these inner movements. This truth is presented most clearly in the Last Supper discourse of Jesus in John's Gospel in the image of the vine and the branches.

> Remain in me, as I remain in you. Just as a branch cannot bear fruit on its own unless it remains on the vine, so neither can you unless you remain in me. I am the vine, you are the branches. Whoever remains in me and I in him will bear much fruit, because without me you can do nothing (Jn 15:4–5).

**Fourth, God transforms our hearts.** Recall that the concentric circles symbolize the interaction of all dimensions of the self; most importantly for our purposes they symbolize the transforming effect of the Spirit on every level of our being — physical and psychological and spiritual. For God's Spirit does not work in a sphere separate from our unique personality: God's Spirit *joins* our spirit; It does not replace it. The human spirit is the center of the self, the source of free choice. From this center every human chooses whether or not to move with God's Spirit. Responding to the Spirit transforms our inner selves — mind, will, imagination, feeling. This means that at every level of our being we can be progressively transformed if we are open to the action of the Spirit.

Granted the all-pervasive action of the Spirit within the self, what is our role? It is absolutely central: we chose whether or not to respond to the movement of the Spirit — God never violates human freedom. This presumes that we are aware of our inner movements and have learned to recognize those from the Spirit from those that are not, and that we want to respond only to those that are from the Spirit. Paul puts it starkly, "Since the Spirit is our life, let us be directed by the Spirit" (Gal 5:25). In short, God initiates all good within us; we choose to respond or not. Note the contrast with the Capitalistic Model mentality; since God is not present, we obviously cannot respond.

### Self-in-God: A Personal Experience

Christian teaching based on the New Testament revelation is unambiguous: the effects of the Spirit are present in every good desire and action. These effects were especially manifest in the aftermath of the auto accidents — more dramatically than I had ever seen at our university. For most of us the recovery period after the deaths extended to the weeks and months after the actual accidents. During this entire time I noted that the Spirit continued to draw us to greater and greater openness to God. Our personal resources were not adequate and many students commented to me that without the help of faith, they could not make it through. Likewise I noted that the Spirit continued to draw us into greater community with one another. To this day I have never observed our community as open to God or as close to one another as we were after the accidents. Our suffering remained; indeed some of us were receiving professional counseling to help us through. But the Spirit was present and we were responding.

During this period I received one of the greatest experiences of God in my own life most unexpectedly. (In presenting it I hope I do not imply that it is only in experiences of similar intensity that we can recognize the Spirit; normally the Spirit works unobtrusively and even unrecognized.) It occurred some weeks after the accidents. I rather suddenly found myself completely exhausted. I had been meeting daily both with individuals and with groups to help process the events. Many, especially those who had been eye-witnesses, were unable to resume normal college life and also unable to sleep. I was attempting to help our students as well as to fulfill my regular duties. I believe I came close to a physical collapse. One Saturday I enrolled at a local church in a day-long Intensive Journal Workshop of Ira Progoff.[6] The Progoff format involves dialogues with key projects, people, events in one's life. The process involves centering, allowing the dialogue to well up from deep within oneself, recording the dialogue in the journal, and finally sharing the experience with the group.

At one point in the day we were asked to dialogue with our primary wisdom figure. I chose Jesus. We (Jesus and I) were dialoguing about my exhaustion and my desire to care for our students as Jesus cared for his people. An image of Jesus the Good Shepherd emerged along with the words of John's Gospel, "The Good Shepherd lays down his life for his sheep." This image was that of the fourth century statue unearthed in the catacomb of St. Callistus in the 1930's. I had seen it in the Vatican Museum in Rome; it had made a great impression on me. It is the first three-dimensional representation of Jesus in Christian history, preceding even the crucifix. During the periods that Christians had to practice their faith in secret because of Roman persecutions the image was safe because it could be mistaken as a perfectly acceptable Roman image of a man bringing an offering of a lamb to a pagan god. This Good Shepherd sculpture depicted a strong young man, beardless, wearing a short Roman tunic and carrying a lamb on his shoulders. In the dialogue I spoke a sentence I have never forgotten: "You carry me and I'll carry your people." And I received a response: "You carry my people and I'll carry you." That was all. I was transformed. I returned to school a different person.

During the weeks that followed the workshop, I continually returned to the image of the Good Shepherd — especially during times of exhaustion. I relived our encounter each time. And I was strengthened to be like Jesus in "laying down my life for my sheep." Each time the Spirit was truly present, acting and transforming my inner self, and I was truly responding. I count the period of the accidents and their aftermath as a time of intense personal transformation through the power of the Spirit in my life. The image remains powerful even today. The awareness of being loved by the Lord strengthens me to become more loving.

A final reflection regarding the two approaches to suffering, the support context and the meaning context. My experience is an example of dealing with suffering within the support context approach. It assumes that God works in our lives normally through the power of the Spirit within us; it approaches God with confidence expecting that the Spirit will be given to help us through our suffering. The approach presumes a model of the self similar to the Scriptural Model of the self. Unfortunately many Christians live with a model of the self that does not acknowledge God's working within our hearts. We approach suffering within the meaning context mindset. We assume that God works in our lives normally by intervening in external events; we expect God to prevent or to mitigate suffering. The result is usually disappointment, frustration and anger at God — as it was initially for Ivan Ilyich. Often this approach assumes a model of the self similar to Capitalistic Model of the self — the model giving God no role in our motivation.

## Capitalistic Model: Self-outside-God

The Self-in-God is surely the model presented in Scripture. Many of us Christians, however, do not recognize the Holy Spirit in our lives. We understand our relationship to God according to the Capitalistic Model of the Self, the Self-outside-God model. In this model the source of all good actions is the self, not God. This model attributes to the self activities that Scripture presents as flowing from the Holy Spirit. We see ourselves as initiating all our good deeds. God enters our understanding of our good actions but only at the end as their rewarder. And God rewards us in two ways. First God rewards us by giving us grace — we understand grace as a spiritual treasury increasing in heaven by our good deeds. Second God rewards us by material prosperity — we understand that the blessings of our life, usually health and wealth, are rewards from God for religious fidelity. I recently met a man who embodied these convictions. All his life he had been a good Christian; and all his life "everything I touched turned to gold." He was convinced that for his fidelity God had blessed him with a loving wife, three children and financial prosperity. Then his wife died of cancer, leaving him to raise three young children. This wasn't supposed to happen. He insisted that his Christian training assured him that fidelity was *always* rewarded with material blessings. God had broken their deal, so he dropped God. When I met him he was looking into Buddhism.

Since this model is so diametrically opposed to Scripture, it has always been intriguing to me how it can get so firmly established in our minds. I believe its causes are both *religious* and *cultural*. Primary among the religious causes is our very image of God. God is presented as a Father in the New Testament. We take this image literally and imagine God as a person existing outside ourselves. Further we assume that this person acts toward us as a parent acts toward a child, rewarding or punishing us according to our behavior. Finally, we conclude that this love is conditional, depending upon our behavior, and see ourselves as called to earn this love by our actions. This view of God distorts the image of God in the New Testament, a God whose love is infinite and unconditional, who never stops loving us no matter how we behave. God's love is freely given, not conditioned by our behavior. The Parable of the Prodigal Son is a fine example: there is nothing the son could do to make his father stop loving him. Likewise with ourselves: we may turn away from God; God never turns away from us. And the *gift* (not *reward*) received is the same one received by the Prodigal Son, the presence of our Father — a gift always freely given, never earned, and given not only at the end of our good actions but also at the beginning and middle. Many Christians have fallen into the trap of believing that the Father's love is dependent upon the performance of good actions and that these actions actually earn a specific reward.

Another religious cause of the Capitalistic Model is our negative view of ourselves. We believe incorrectly that because of our sinfulness God could not possibly dwell within us. Preserving God's holiness demands keeping God apart from our sinful human condition. We do not realize that even with our limitations Jesus lives with us and calls us to be one with him as he and the Father are one, thus giving us a dignity almost beyond imagination.

A further religious cause, especially for Catholics, is a misunderstanding of how we are saved. Are we saved by faith or by good works? Protestants traditionally hold the first; Catholics the second. But this is a false dichotomy; both are vital. The Scriptural Model highlights that good works flow from the Spirit received by faith and baptism. Further, Catholics have frequently not grasped that the "reward" flowing from good works — the "merit" or "indulgence" — is nothing less than a deeper union with the Lord. By responding to the Spirit and doing good deeds we have deepened our openness to this union. We Catholics had erroneously turned grace into a quantifiable substance stored up outside of ourselves in heaven.

And there are many *cultural* influences contributing to the Capitalistic Model approach to God. The primary influence is secularism. We live in a thoroughly secular culture. Our culture does not support a religious view of society nor a religious view of the person. Our societal institutions rarely advert to the reality of God, and individual motivation is seen solely through the eyes of secular psychologists with insights from faith rarely if ever added. Religion when recognized at all is relegated to the private and personal sphere, reinforced at best by our families and religious institutions. And frequently God's activity even within this personal realm is understood inaccurately through the Capitalistic Model, thereby giving God no real role in our motivation.

Another cultural influence is our capitalistic economic system. This economic system reinforces the Capitalistic Model's conviction that

God's relationship to us is conditioned by our behavior. Hence God's distribution of *grace* is conditioned by behavior. Just as an employer compensates an employee by financial rewards, giving financial raises to the industrious and withholding them from the less productive, so also does God compensate us for our good actions by giving or withholding grace. Further God's distribution of *material prosperity* is also conditioned by our behavior. Sociologists concerned with showing the influence of culture on religion have described what is called "the Puritan ethic." This ethic arose in Europe in the seventeenth century with the rise of the new capitalistic economy. It asserts that God distributes blessings unequally, giving material prosperity as a reward for faithfulness only to the righteous — indeed for some, prosperity is a sign of being predestined by God for eternal salvation.[8] It is obvious how this capitalistic mentality can subtly reinforce a view of God whose love is conditioned by behavior. And before we ever leave home and enter the marketplace, the rewards and punishments involved in healthy discipline at home and in school have also subtly though deeply influenced our view of God: in life you get only what you earn.

A further cultural influence supporting the Capitalistic Model is our "Yankee Independence" — perhaps the American frontier experience makes this attitude more prevalent among Americans than among Europeans. Something in us fears any type of dependence, be this with one another or with God. We feel that all dependence is demeaning. My students frequently react negatively when I explain that we can do good deeds only with God's help. They feel the dignity of their human nature has been impugned. I explain that God has created us to be fully actualized only when we act in the Spirit and that we act below the dignity of our being when our actions are not transformed by the Spirit. Yet for Americans, the cowboy riding alone out of town remains an ideal — self-reliant, independent, needing nothing and no one, not even God.

The Capitalistic Model of the self subtly reinforces the meaning context approach to suffering. Since this model of the self does not recognize the power of God working within the self, it looks for God outside the self in the events of creation and history, especially in the material blessings of health and wealth. When these blessings are absent the believer spontaneously asks, "Why are You doing this to me, O God?" The answer to this question is never given. The result is increased suffering and frequently alienation from God.

It is important to acknowledge the persuasiveness of the Capitalistic Model mentality in our own selves. I help students reach this self-awareness simply by asking them to give an example of a recent good deed and then explain it according to the two models. Most are incapable of doing this. They begin looking for some dramatic experience of transcendence in recent days and, not surprisingly, find none. Again I ask for any good deed from recent days — no dramatic experience needed. Frequently a male student will remember that on the way to school he stopped on the interstate highway to help someone change a flat tire. I point out the similarity to the Parable of the Good Samaritan. Recall that the Good Samaritan stopped to help a person, presumably a Jew, who had been robbed, beaten and left half-dead on the highway. The student haltingly explains that in the Scriptural Model God initiated the desire to help and he responded — but not for a moment does he believe God was really involved. Continuing he explains that in the Capitalistic Model he initiated the good deed with no help from God, though God was doubtless pleased — this is what he believes. At this point all are forced to deal with their habitual assumptions of God's work in their lives. Is God really involved somehow with these very ordinary events? The students have intellectually understood the lesson, but their life-long assumptions prohibit them from applying it to daily experience.

### The Holy Spirit and Christian *Spirit*uality

Let's return to the central question of this chapter: "How do we *expect* God to act in our lives now?" Given that God creates and sustains the world in existence, I believe that the New Testament teaches that since Pentecost we can expect God to work in our lives normally through the Holy Spirit. Indeed Christian *spirit*uality can be understood simply as our attempt to live our entire lives in response to God's Spirit — a book on suffering is really a book on spirituality since it applies Christian understanding of the Spirit to times of suffering. The following four assertions get to the heart of Christian spirituality and provide a solid foundation for the rest of this book.

**First, Christian spirituality is love centered, focusing on love of God and love of neighbor, or more accurately, love of neighbor for the love of God.** Love is the primary effect of God's presence within us, for God is love. Recall the Gospel accounts of "the great commandment." In Luke's account a scholar of the law stood up to test Jesus, asking Jesus a crucial question.

> "Teacher, what must I do to inherit eternal life?" Jesus said to him, "What is written in the law? How do you read it?" He said in reply, "You shall love the Lord, your God, with all your heart, with all your being, with all your strength, and with all your mind, and your neighbor as yourself." He replied to him, "You have answered correctly; do this and you shall live" (Lk 10:25–28).

In response to a further question "Who is my neighbor?" Luke continues with the Parable of the Good Samaritan. The Parable illustrates two important aspects of Jesus' teaching: first that love is shown by practical actions serving our neighbor's need and second that love goes out to everyone — strangers, friends, even enemies like Samaritans (Jews and Samaritans were enemies). In short, Christian spirituality is other-centered and not self-centered, not merely a method for getting ourselves to heaven. The Gospels assure us that if we love one another we don't have to worry about getting to heaven.

**Second, Christian spirituality is concerned primarily with daily action.** Often we Christians think that Christian spirituality has more to do with love for God expressed through daily prayer than with love for others shown in actions. We assume we are leading good Christian lives if we are faithful to regular personal prayer and weekly worship. Jesus, while never undervaluing prayer and worship of his Father, clearly witnesses to the centrality of serving others. Often his withdrawing from the crowds to pray seems to guide and strengthen him in his mission. Indeed, in his teaching Jesus often connected the two commandments, asking us to show our love for God by loving one another: Whatever you did to the least of these you did to me! In short, daily actions are as important as daily prayer.

**Third, Christian spirituality is concerned with the quality of heart underlying our actions.** Often we feel that the performance of an action, be it prayer to God or service to others, automatically fulfills the commandments to love God and others. Jesus teaches differently. The Gospels present Jesus as having the greatest difficulty with a group of people who perfectly fulfilled the commandments externally, the Pharisees. Jesus refers to them as whitened-sepulchers because while appearing externally to be faithful to the commandments, internally they violated the very essence of the commandments — love. Paul gives us a list of the qualities of heart that reflect the presence of the Spirit: love, joy, peace, patience, kindness, generosity, faithfulness, gentleness, self-control. He contrasts these qualities with certain actions marking the absence of the Spirit: immorality, impurity, hatreds, rivalry, jealousy, envy, selfishness, warning that such acts will not inherit the kingdom of heaven (Gal 5:19-23). In short, the quality of heart underlying our actions is as important as the external performance of actions.

**Fourth, Christian *spiri*tuality is a response to the Spirit.** The Gospel teaches that all love has its origin in God. When we live in love we live in God; it's that simple. The power to love derives ultimately from God's Spirit. John's teaching is clear and bold.

> Beloved, let us love one another, because love is of God; everyone who loves is begotten of God and knows God. Whoever is without love does not know God, for God is love. . . . Beloved, if God so loved us, we also must love one another. No one has ever seen God. Yet, if we love one another, God remains in us, and his love is brought to perfection in us (1 Jn 4:7–8, 11–12).

Choosing to love is choosing to respond to God's Spirit. But it's not even necessary to advert explicitly to this desire to love. Recall the Last Judgment scene in Matthew. Those welcomed by the Son of Man had no recollection of serving God in giving food to the hungry and drink to the thirsty. The Son of Man assures them it doesn't matter for as long as they genuinely served others, they served God. Very simply: wherever there is love in the world, there is God. And Vatican II assures us that through the Incarnation the Spirit is united in some sense to every human being. Therefore this Spirit of God is present and working not only in Christians but in all people in all cultures.

> All this holds true not only for Christians but for all people of good will in whose hearts grace works in an unseen way. For since Christ died for all people, and since the ultimate vocation of humanity is in fact one, and divine, we ought to believe that the Holy Spirit in a manner known only to God offers to every person the possibilities of being associated with the paschal mystery.[9]

The key question for conscientious Christians becomes: "How do we know whether or not we are responding to the Spirit?" I am suggesting that the simplest criterion is the presence or absence of the desire to love in our hearts. **To the degree that our hearts are free and are moving toward the desire to love and serve God and others, we are responding to the Spirit; to the degree that our hearts are moving away from this desire, we are not.**[10] (Human motivation is immensely complex, and it is difficult to get in touch with deep often unconscious levels of our motivation; yet I believe that this conscious desire to love remains our best operative criterion.) Any approach to dealing with suffering must be set within this context. Christian spirituality is our effort to arrange our lives to live in response to the Spirit and so to love God and others with our entire heart, soul, mind and body — in good times and in troubled times.

### Strong, Loving and Wise

We Christians are challenged to love and serve God and our neighbor during all the moments of our lives. This challenge is experienced most acutely in times of suffering. Suffering tends to self-center us. During suffering we are tempted to excuse ourselves from the Gospel mandate, withdraw from others and indulge in self-pity. Consequently at no time do we need the help of the Spirit more to remain faithful to our calling. And responding to the Spirit during suffering can become the key moment of transformation in our Christian lives. It was for Ivan.

The New Testament presents many examples showing the transformation that occurs through the power of the Spirit. Perhaps the most dramatic witness is the descent of the Spirit upon the disciples at Pentecost. It transformed them from cowards to martyrs for the Gospel. Paul reminded Timothy that he too had received this Spirit; perhaps he needed reminding because the hardships were getting to him.

> For this reason, I remind you to stir into flame the gift of God bestowed when my hands were laid on you. The Spirit God has given us is no cowardly spirit, but rather one that makes us *strong, loving, and wise.* Therefore, never be ashamed of your testimony to our Lord, nor of me, a prisoner for his sake; but with the strength which comes from God bear your share of the hardship which the gospel entails (2 Tim 1:6–8, italics mine).[11]

Openness to the Spirit makes Christians *strong* in living the Gospel at all times, and especially during hardships. Openness to the Spirit makes us *loving,* freeing us from a sinful self-centeredness and enabling us to live the two great commandments. And openness to the Spirit makes us *wise,* enabling us to grasp the wisdom of God, even if it is the wisdom of the cross!

> For the Jews demand signs and Greeks look for wisdom, but we proclaim Christ crucified, a stumbling block to Jews and foolishness to Gentiles, but to those who are called, Jews and Greeks alike, Christ the power of God and the wisdom of God. For the foolishness of God is wiser than human wisdom, and the weakness of God is stronger than human strength (1 Cor 1:22–25).

Perhaps it was his own transformation through suffering that enabled Paul to exclaim, "I have been crucified with Christ; yet I live, no longer I, but Christ lives in me" (Gal 2:19–20). This transformation is the goal of Christian spirituality.

With this background on New Testament spirituality we can now return to our main topic: suffering. We will focus upon the two specifically religious approaches to dealing with suffering described in Chapter I. Chapter III illustrates the meaning context approach by examining its use in the Old Testament. Since the meaning context approach is not centered on the Spirit, our discussion on the Spirit will be interrupted. Chapters IV through VI, however, return to the support context approach, examining its use in the New Testament and focusing upon the role of the Holy Spirit. But since the meaning context approach is the approach used initially by most Christians to cope with suffering, we begin with it.

## REFLECTION QUESTIONS

1. How do you *expect* God to work in your daily life? Explain your position in light of the four approaches given.

2. Are you comfortable with the key insight of the Scriptural Model that the Holy Spirit is the initiator of all good thoughts, words and deeds

and that we respond to the Spirit? Discuss. Give examples of recent good deeds and explain them according to the two models of the self.

3. In general what has this chapter added to your realization of the effects of the Holy Spirit in Christian life? How has it affected your previous understanding? Are you comfortable with your insights? Explain.

4. Do you recognize elements of the Capitalistic Model in your understanding of your relationship with God? Explain. How is this model reinforced by our culture and frequently even by our religions?

5. Review a recent day examining the quality of your heart for the presence and absence of the Holy Spirit (use the desire to love as the sign of your response to the presence of the Spirit). Which actions are usually done under the influence of the Spirit? Which are not?

6. Give specific experiences from your past life of the Holy Spirit making you strong, loving and wise. Has this happened during times of suffering? Did you recognize God at the time?

# III.  WHY ME, O GOD?
## OLD TESTAMENT INSIGHTS

"An Act of God Is a Hard Act to Follow" — so read the headline of the American Red Cross brochure seeking additional contributions to aid victims of a devastating Florida hurricane. The day I discovered that brochure in my grocery bag, the headlines of the local paper read, "Biggest Question of Storm: Why? Floridians Wonder Why Bad Hurricanes Happen to Good People." The article quoted victims' reflections on the disaster: "I think God is testing our faith; I still believe in Him because I'm alive." And, "This is what South Florida gets when the President refuses to let Haitian refugees into our country." Clearly the immediate reaction of these hurricane victims was to seek some help from their faith in dealing with their losses. And so they spontaneously began looking for God's reasons for sending the disaster asking the age-old question of believers, "Why is God doing this to us?" Their reactions echoed the reaction of my university community at the deaths of our students. Their faith response falls clearly within the meaning context mindset described in Chapter I, namely, God is the direct cause of every event and God has specific reasons for each suffering.

But looking for God's reasons for sending suffering is not limited to spontaneous popular reactions. Carlo Carretto, a highly respected spiritual writer holding a doctorate in philosophy, uses the meaning context approach to suffering in his popular book *Why, O Lord? The Inner Meaning of Suffering*.[1] Carretto joined the Little Brothers of Jesus at the age of forty-four and eventually moved to Algeria to live among the poor on the edges of the Sahara desert. As a young man before joining the Little Brothers he enjoyed mountain climbing. He explains in his book that he dreamed of serving God by going to the Alps and living with the Alpine teams whose work was rescuing people caught in storms. But on one hike before implementing his dream he experienced problems with his leg. A nurse friend gave him an injection as a remedy for the pain. The result was disastrous.

> And with the best of intentions my friend stuck a needle in my thigh and injected me with a paralyzing poison. In less that twenty-four hours my leg was useless.
> He had made a mistake.
> He'd used the wrong vial. . . .
> I was paralyzed for life.[2]

Carretto, now paralyzed for life, wonders whether it would not be better to have a world without suffering, without "cripples" like himself.

> The answer has become clearer with the passing of the years.
> No! Without suffering, without tears, without death, the world would be all the uglier. Worse still, mankind would be wickeder, you might even say diabolical.
> If people are so wicked as it is under the heavy hand of the Crippler — without the crippling they would be unbearable![3]

God could have made a world without suffering. But God willed suffering.

> It is no good saying that God does not will the evil; that human guilt and an ecology in shambles are to blame for our sufferings.
> That won't wash!
> I like Jacob's solution. It seems simpler to me.
> It's God himself who crippled me.[4]

But God wills suffering only for our growth.

> But precisely in wounding me he draws out the best in me.
> If I were not wounded — how unbearable I should be in my fiendish security! How sure of myself!
> Wounded, I remain calm and learn to weep. Weeping I learn to understand others, I learn the blessedness of poverty.[5]

Carretto emphatically denies that God ever causes suffering as a punishment for sin: "God punishes no one, and now that I have come to know him a little I am ashamed of a time when I immaturely thought of pain as God's punishment."[6]

Carretto's reflections, coming not from disinterested philosophical speculation but from his own struggle to understand God's role in his suffering, are compelling. Though I disagree with his conclusions, in no way do I want to demean them. His writings have provided consolation for many, enabling them to deal better with their suffering. They superbly illustrate the meaning context approach to dealing with suffering: God is the direct cause of every suffering — even accidental suffering; and God causes suffering for specific reasons — to help us grow.

But Carretto also employs the support context approach. His writings reflect his own profound experience of God's presence and strength. Like many of us he spontaneously assumes that God is the direct cause of his suffering while simultaneously seeking God's help to deal with it. I have distinguished the two approaches for purposes of discussion but most often they exist together.

Our discussion now moves away from the support context approach and centers upon the meaning context approach. While both approaches are present in each Testament, the Old Testament approaches suffering predominantly within the meaning context mindset. It is crucial to understand this emphasis to appreciate more fully its difference from the New Testament emphasis. We examine the Old Testament looking first at the dominant tradition, then at some of its modifications, and finally at the challenge to the entire tradition presented by the Book of Job.[7] In no way do I want to deny the presence of the support context in the Old Testament. I focus on the meaning context because it is the dominant Jewish approach to integrating perceived disorders within the Jewish faith vision.

## Meaning Context: Suffering as Punishment for Sin

Two questions haunted our students after the tragic automobile accidents: "What have we done to deserve this?" "Is God punishing us?" These are the same questions asked by sufferers throughout the Old Testament. And the dominant Old Testament tradition responds to the questions affirmatively: God sends suffering as a punishment for sin. How does the Old Testament reach this conclusion about God's relationship to suffering?

"Hear, O Israel, the Lord is our God, the Lord alone! Therefore you shall love the Lord, your God, with all your heart, and with all your soul, and with all your strength" (Dt 6:4–5). So begins the creed recited twice daily by pious Jews even today. Since Yahweh had chosen the Israelites from among all the peoples of the earth to be a special people, the Israelites owed Yahweh their entire allegiance. The first of the ten commandments given Moses on Sinai was unequivocal.

> I, the Lord, am your God, who brought you out of the land of Egypt, that place of slavery. You shall not have other gods besides me. You shall not carve idols for yourselves in the shape of anything in the sky above or on the earth below or in the waters beneath the earth; you shall not bow down before them or worship them. For I, the Lord, your God, am a jealous God, inflicting punishment for their fathers' wickedness on the children of those who hate me down to the third and fourth generation; but bestowing mercy down to the thousandth generation, on the children of those who love me and keep my commandments (Ex 20:2–6).

And Yahweh not only chooses the Israelites as a special people but Yahweh acts through creation and history to care for them: the call to Abraham, the deliverance from slavery in Egypt, the guidance through the desert for forty years, the victories in battles for possession of the Promised Land, the anointed kings and prophets — as well as the covenant made with Moses and the Hebrews on Sinai.

Yahweh is a merciful and loving God, but Yahweh is also a just God. Yahweh must act justly even when dealing with the Chosen People. And so the first commandment prescribes consequences flowing from observance of the covenant — punishment and blessing in accordance with fidelity. How then do the Israelites explain God's relationship to suffering? The Israelite solution is quite simple: God has arranged the world to insure that both blessings and curses occur in accordance with covenant fidelity; the just are rewarded with prosperity and the sinners are punished with adversity. This holds true for Israel as a people as well as for individual Israelites.

A brief note on what is sometimes called "the doctrine of divine retribution." Formerly scripture scholars had suggested that "divine retribution" occurred through a judicial process in which Yahweh stood outside the created order, passed judgment according to the norms of the covenant and rewarded or punished accordingly. Scholars today, however, take a slightly different approach. They point out that rewards and punishments are built into the fabric of creation by God; "human action takes place in an arena of built-in consequences, set in motion, speeded up, and finally brought to completion by Yahweh's active involvement."[8] This connection between acts and consequences inherent in the very order of creation is found in the Old Testament as well as in other Near Eastern texts. One scholar expresses the emerging consensus.

> Whoever does what is right conforms to the created order . . . and hence stands under the blessing. Whoever acts wrongly must in some special way bear the consequences of this deed and thus stands under the curse. In some ancient Near Eastern texts, as well as some in the OT, the relation between acts and consequence is effected automatically, by inner necessity. In other texts the (creator-) deity is the executor. There is no substantial contradiction between the two, so long as the inner force of the order of creation and the action of the creator god are not differentiated.[9]

But it is important to point out that the two approaches are complementary, not contradictory.

> Is it necessary to choose between these two points of view of retribution, or could both of them have been operative in Israel's experience? Probably the latter. There is something profound in the thought that evil somehow corrupts and that the good will not be without its effect. Moderns might call this "poetic justice." But one cannot exclude the basic biblical understanding of the all-pervasive causality of God in human affairs.[10]

Both views support the Israelite belief in "divine retribution": God is faithful to the covenant made on Mount Sinai.

The first five books of the Bible, the Pentateuch, establish the context for interpreting God's activity toward Israel. This covenant theology is found throughout the Bible; it is the basic model for interpreting all God's actions in Jewish history. The Historical Books of the Old Testament, Joshua through Kings, reflect this covenant tradition. The so-called "deuteronomic historian," the editor-compiler of these books, was guided by this covenant theology in his presentation of Israelite history. The Book of Deuteronomy gives its classical expression:

> Thus, then, shall it be: if you continue to heed the voice of the Lord, your God, and are careful to observe all his commandments which I enjoin on you today, the Lord, your God will raise you high above all the nations of the earth. When you hearken to the voice of the Lord, your God, all these blessings will come upon you and overwhelm you (Dt 28:1–2).

The author then concretizes the way the Israelites can expect to be blessed if they are faithful to the covenant: you will be blessed in the city and in the country; you will be blessed in the fruit of your womb, the produce of your soil and in your livestock; and the Lord will beat down your enemies before you. But then the messages abruptly change and the author presents the consequences of infidelity to the covenant: "But if you do not hearken to the voice of the Lord, your God, and are not careful to observe all his commandments which I enjoin on you today, all these curses shall come upon you and overwhelm you" (Dt 28:15). And the entire list of blessings is systematically converted to curses: you will be cursed in the city and in the country, and so on.

Likewise the Prophetic Books reflect the covenant perspective. The prophets Isaiah and Jeremiah interpret the conquering of the Northern Kingdom of Israel by the Assyrians and the Southern Kingdom of Judah by the Babylonians as God's punishment for infidelity to the covenant. The opening chapter of the Book of Isaiah is typical of these prophetic oracles.

> Hear, O heavens, and listen, O earth, for the Lord speaks:
> Sons have I raised and reared, but they have disowned me!
> An ox knows its owner, and an ass, its master's manger;
> But Israel does not know, my people has not understood.
> Ah! sinful nation, people laden with wickedness, evil race, corrupt
>     children!
> They have forsaken the Lord, spurned the Holy One of Israel,
>     apostatized.
> Where would you yet be struck, you that rebel again and again? . . .
> Your country is waste, your cities burnt with fire;

Your land before your eyes strangers devour (a waste like Sodom
  overthrown) —
And daughter Zion is left like a hut in a vineyard,
Like a shed in a melon patch, like a city blockaded (Is 1:2–8).

The story of Jonah and the Ninevites is an example of covenant theology familiar to all: 1. The Ninevites violate the covenant; 2. God raises
up the prophet Jonah to threaten the Ninevites with misfortune unless
they repent; 3. They repent; 4. God withdraws the punishment.

> The word of the Lord came to Jonah a second time: "Set out for the
> great city of Nineveh and announce to it the message I will give to
> you." . . . Jonah began his journey through the city, and had gone but
> a single day's walk announcing, "Forty days more and Nineveh shall
> be destroyed," when the people of Nineveh believed in God; they pro-
> claimed a fast and all of them, great and small, put on sackcloth. . . .
> When God saw by their actions how they had turned from this evil
> way, he repented of the evil that he had threatened to do to them; he
> did not carry it out (Jon 3:1–10).

The most familiar Old Testament texts reflecting the covenant perspective are in the Book of Psalms. Since the psalms were written over
some six hundred years they give testimony to Hebrew mentality through
most of the Old Testament period. Commentators on Psalm 1 indicate
that the psalm stands as a preface to the entire Book of Psalms, with its
references to the way of the just and the way of the wicked.

> Happy those who do not follow the counsel of the wicked
> Nor go the way of sinners, nor sit in the company of scoffers.
> Rather, the law of the Lord is their joy; God's law they study day and
>   night.
> They are like a tree planted near streams of water, that yields its fruit in
>   season;
> Its leaves never wither; whatever they do prospers.
>
> But not the wicked! They are like chaff driven by the wind.
> Therefore the wicked will not survive judgment, nor will sinners in the
>   assembly of the just.
> The Lord watches over the way of the just, but the way of the wicked
>   leads to ruin.

Psalm 37 is another familiar expression of the covenant perspective.

> Do not be provoked by evildoers;
>     do not envy those who do wrong.
> Like the grass they wither quickly;
>     like green plants they wilt away.
>
> Trust in the Lord and do good,
>     that you may dwell in the land and live secure,
> Find your delight in the Lord
>     who will give you your heart's desire (Ps 37:1–4).

Old Testament texts such as those cited above clearly support the meaning context approach to suffering: God is the direct cause of all events and God causes sufferings for specific reasons. God works through the events of history and creation acting according to the covenant stipulations: rewarding the just with blessings and punishing the unjust with misfortunes. The revelation on Sinai remains the fundamental criterion for interpreting God's actions toward the Jews.

This pattern of interpreting historical events is so central to Jewish tradition that it remains the focus even today for Jewish interpretation of history. Secular Jews — Jews not believing in the existence of God — frequently ascribe their unbelief to an inability to reconcile the events of Jewish history such as the Holocaust with the existence of a caring God. Religious Jews also continue to grapple with suffering within this tradition. Rabbi Harold Kushner's *When Bad Things Happen to Good People* is the best known contemporary wrestling with the problem of suffering. Rabbi Kushner admits that he himself never seriously questioned this reward and punishment perspective until forced to by his son's fatal disease.

> Like most people, my wife and I had grown up with an image of God as an all-wise, all-powerful parent figure who would treat us as our earthly parents did, or even better. If we were obedient and deserving, He would reward us. If we got out of line, He would discipline us, reluctantly but firmly. He would protect us from being hurt or from hurting ourselves, and would see to it that we got what we deserved in life.[11]

In the aftermath of our campus tragedies, the questions most often put to me in private were: "What have we done to deserve this?" "Why is God doing this to us?" The questions imply both that God was the direct cause of the automobile accidents and that God caused them as punishment for sin. In attempting to understand this particular Christian approach to suffering it is essential to acknowledge its prevalence in the Old Testament. The Capitalistic Model of the self described in Chapter II is relevant because it looks outside the self for evidence of God's blessings. This model sees God rewarding fidelity by giving material prosperity to the faithful. It should be added that the Capitalistic Model is only partially applicable to the Jewish tradition. In the dominant Jewish tradition there is no belief in grace nor in an afterlife; consequently the good can be rewarded solely with material prosperity and only in this life.[12]

## Meaning Context: Modifications

The meaning context mindset assumes that God is the direct cause of suffering and attempts to handle suffering by discovering God's reasons for sending it. The Old Testament sees God as insuring — through the created order or through direct intervention — that suffering is a punishment for infidelity to the covenant. But the punishment is always for the purpose of helping the Jews return to God, never for any arbitrary vindictiveness on God's part. Since Yahweh remains loving and merciful even while being just, adversities are signals to the Jews that they have strayed from covenant fidelity and so must repent. But the Old Testament also presents three other reasons why God causes suffering, though all three remain very minor themes in Jewish tradition. Some of these same reasons for suffering troubled our students in the aftermath of the auto accidents.

**God sends suffering to help us grow.** Though this reason is related to punishment, God's intention here is different. Suffering occurs not because of actual infidelity but rather because of barriers within us inhibiting us from serving the Lord fully. Such sufferings are a blessings because they enlarge our capacity for loving God and others. This type of suffering is more aptly called *discipline* than *punishment.* The most widely known passage illustrating this reason is in the Book of Proverbs.

The discipline of the Lord, my son, disdain not;
spurn not his reproof;
For whom the Lord loves he reproves,
and he chastises the son he favors (Prov 3:11–12).

This passage is familiar to Christians because it is quoted almost verbatim in the Epistle to the Hebrews.

My son, do not disdain the discipline of the Lord
or lose heart when reproved by him;
for whom the Lord loves, he disciplines;
he scourges every son he acknowledges (Heb 12:5–6).

Carlo Carretto shares this belief.

**God sends suffering to test our faith.** Suffering exposes the depth of our commitment to God — it helps *us* understand for presumably God already knows. The test of Abraham is the classic example. God asks Abraham to sacrifice his son Isaac. Is Abraham willing? Does Abraham love God more than Isaac? Job is another example. God gives Satan permission to test Job by taking away Job's prosperity, his children, his health, his reputation. Will Job's faith in God remain strong in spite of losing his prosperity, or is Job's faith and love of God built upon having these blessings? Both Abraham and Job passed the test.

I recently witnessed a modern-day Job comfort himself using this reason for his suffering. He was a minister in his early thirties who had just received his first pastorate, a small rural parish. He discovered he had cancer only after his wife had become pregnant with their fifth child. For over a year he and his wife fought the cancer courageously with all means available. During his final months he shared with me his belief that God sent his suffering as a test to give him the opportunity to prove his faith; the phrase he continually used was, "Why me? Try me." Even in semi-delirium of his final days he repeated the phrase, "Why me? Try me." He also passed the test.

**Finally God chooses certain people — individuals or groups — to suffer with the intention that their suffering will be redemptive for themselves and for their communities.** The Book of Isaiah is the classic presentation. Chapters 40–55 of Isaiah, often called the Book of Consolation, were written while the Israelites were in exile in Babylon, having been defeated in a war with the Babylonians and driven out of Jerusalem. The Jews were displaced persons in a foreign land, yearning to return to their homeland. Yet they remained aware they were God's chosen people. How could they understand the tragedy that had happened to them? A prophecy assured them that their defeat need not be a catastrophe but could be an opportunity. If they accept their misfortune as deserved because of their infidelity to the covenant — again the traditional reason for suffering — their suffering in exile could become the occasion for a whole new rebirth for their people. The prophecies speak about a servant of the Lord chosen by the Lord to suffer for the people but whose sufferings would eventually save the people. There are various interpretations of who this servant is, but most agree that the Servant can be considered the entire Jewish community in Babylon — all of whom were suffering to atone for the previous sins of their people.

> See my servant shall prosper, he shall be raised high and greatly exalted. . . . He grew up like a sapling before him, like a shoot from the parched earth; there was in him no stately bearing to make us look at him, nor appearance that would attract us to him. He was spurned and avoided by men, a man of suffering, accustomed to infirmity, one of those from whom men hide their faces, spurned, and we hold him in no esteem. Yet it was our infirmities that he bore, our sufferings that he endured, while we thought of him as stricken, as one smitten by God and afflicted. But he was pierced for our offenses, crushed for our sins; upon him was the chastisement that makes us whole, by his stripes we were healed. We had all gone astray like sheep, each following his own way; but the Lord laid upon him the guilt of us all (Is 52:13 – 53:6).

The Jews were eventually released from Babylon and allowed to return to Jerusalem. This return in the interpretation of many fulfilled the prophecies of Isaiah. Christians, it should be noted, while assenting to the above interpretation of Isaiah also see in the text a reference to Jesus: Jesus is the servant of the Lord by whose suffering we are redeemed.

The Old Testament presents an approach to handling suffering that looks for the reasons suffering occurs. Since God is the cause of all that happens — either through the created order itself or through direct intervention — God must be the cause of suffering. Dealing with suffering involves seeking the reasons for God's action. As these reasons become known suffering can more easily be accepted. What had been perceived as a disorder threatening to faith vision can now be perceived as ordered and integrated within that vision. From beginning to end the Old Testament is dominated by the view that through the created order itself or through direct divine intervention suffering occurs for specific reasons: punishment for sin, discipline to foster growth, test of fidelity, opportunity for redeeming others. The following expanded diagram applies the meaning context paradigm explained in Chapter I to Old Testament insights.

It is now necessary to examine the challenge presented to this Old Testament approach by the Book of Job.[13] Please note that in one aspect the Book of Job does remain within the meaning context approach: it acknowledges that God is indeed the direct cause of Job's suffering. It departs from the dominant tradition, however, in denying that Job's sufferings are a punishment for sin.

### The Book of Job: Challenging the Meaning Context Approach

An examination of the Book of Job is crucial for a comprehensive view of suffering as found in the Old Testament. The Book of Job rein-

### Diagram 3
### Old Testament Approach to Suffering

**Meaning Context:
Why, O God?**

1. God is the direct cause of suffering
2. God causes suffering for a specific reason

Perceived Disorder: Faith-Threatening

Perceived Order: Faith-Integrated

| **Jewish Tradition:** | **Book of Job:** |
|---|---|
| 1. Punishment for sin | Incomprehensible |
| 2. Education for growth | |
| 3. Test of faith | |
| 4. Redemptive for others | |

forces the Jewish conviction that God is the cause of every event and that God causes suffering for a specific reason. The entire book focuses on Job's struggles to find God's reasons for causing his sufferings. Job, ever claiming innocence before God, challenges the assertion of his friends that his sufferings are punishment for his sins. What is at stake here is nothing less than the central tenet of covenant theology, namely, suffering as caused by God as a punishment for sin. The question is not *whether* God is causing the suffering — this is assumed — but why God is causing an *innocent* person to suffer. In the final chapter Job's innocence is affirmed by God and so the central tenet of the Old Testament approach is challenged.

The story of the Book of Job is familiar to all. The Prologue presents the context for the story. The main character, Job, most likely a legendary and not historical figure, is defined in the opening verse as "a blameless and upright man who feared God and avoided evil." He remains throughout the Prologue the type of the "innocent sufferer." Job has experienced all the blessing promised to those faithful to the covenant, and God is proud of Job's fidelity. Satan, however, believes that Job's fidelity is motivated by self-interest rather than by love of God. God denies this and allows Satan to test the sincerity of Job's faith by progressively taking away all Job's blessings, his wealth, children, health. The Book of Job is a classic example of God's sending suffering to test the faith of believers. Through all this, however, the author carefully notes that Job did nothing sinful; Job remained faithful to God: "The Lord gave and the Lord has taken away; blessed be the name of the Lord" (Jb 1:21).

The dialogues between Job and his friends in Chapters 3–37 present Job's attempt to cope with his suffering by applying the interpretation of covenant theology. Job's friends reiterate the covenant theology: Job is experiencing misfortunes; therefore Job must have sinned — perhaps Job just can't recall the sin, perhaps it is Job's questioning God's ways that is his sin. Job vehemently denies that he has sinned in a way deserving of such misfortune. Throughout his protest Job insists that God remains all wise and all powerful and wants only to know God's intentions in sending misfortunes so he can better accept them. Since he is certain he has not sinned, punishment for sin cannot be the reason. In these chapters Job's attempt to use the traditional Jewish meaning context to cope with suffering reaches total frustration.

Chapters 38–42 move in an entirely different direction. God inter-venes, thus breaking the theological impasse between Job and his friends. In two separate addresses God confirms control over the events of Job's life, astonished that Job could even presume to question this.

> Who is this that obscures divine plans with words of ignorance?
> Gird up your loins now, like a man; I will question you and you tell me
>     the answers!
> Where were you when I founded the earth? Tell me if you have
>     understanding?
> Who determined its size; do you know? Who stretched out the
>     measuring line for it?
> Into what were its pedestals sunk, and who laid the cornerstone,
> While the morning stars sang in chorus and all the sons of God shouted
>     for joy? (Jb 38:2–7).

> Gird up your loins now, like a man. I will question you, and you tell me
>     the answers!
> Would you refuse to acknowledge my right?
> Would you condemn me that you may be justified?
> Have you an arm like that of God, or can you thunder with a voice like his?
> Adorn yourself with grandeur and majesty,
> and array yourself with glory and splendor.
> Let loose the fury of your wrath; tear down the wicked and shatter them.
> Bring down the haughty with a glance; bury them in the dust together;
> in the hidden world imprison them.
> Then will I too acknowledge that your own right hand can save you
>     (Jb 40:7–14).

God's speeches ask Job to reflect upon the grandeur of creation. If God is capable of creating such marvels, shouldn't God be capable of run-ning the world — and by implication Job's life? What has Job done to give him the right to challenge God's competence? But significantly, God does not disclose the reason for Job's suffering.

Then in the two responses following God's accusations, Job repents of questioning God's ways.

> Behold I am of little account; what can I answer you?
> I put my hand over my mouth.
> Though I have spoken once, I will not do so again;
> though twice, I will do so no more (Jb 40:4–5).

And with an intensity flowing from a radically new experience of God, Job reiterates his retraction.

> I know that you can do all things, and that no purpose of yours can be
>    hindered.
> I have dealt with great things I do not understand;
> things too wonderful for me, which I cannot know.
> I had heard of you by word of mouth, but now my eye has seen you.
> Therefore I disown what I have said, and repent in dust and ashes
>    (Jb 42:2–6).

Never for a moment does Job deny God's control over events. Rather Job acknowledges this control anew and repents of challenging God's ways, recognizing how inadequate he is to grasp the designs of such a God. Job now abandons his attempt to understand God's intentions and humbles himself in God's presence — a presence manifested more intensely than Job had ever known: "I had heard of you by word of mouth, but now my eye has seen you." And Job is wiser. Most scholars agree with James Crenshaw's assertion.

> What, then, has Job learned from this first-hand encounter with God? Perhaps the first thing he discovered concerned the mistaken reason for Job's quest. The consuming passion for vindication suddenly presented itself as ludicrous once the courageous rebel stood in God's presence. By maintaining complete silence on this singular issue which had brought Job to a confrontation with his maker, God taught his servant the error in assuming that the universe operated according to a principle of rationality. Once that putative principle of order collapsed before the divine freedom, the need for personal vindication vanished as well, since God's anger and favor show no positive correspondence with the human acts of villainy or virtue.[14]

In the Epilogue Job's fortunes are completely restored. Speaking directly to one of Job's friends God vindicates Job and criticizes the friends: "I am angry with you and your two friends; for you have not spoken rightly concerning me, as has my servant Job" (Jb 42:7). Differing from the dominant Old Testament tradition the Epilogue asserts that when suffering occurs it need not be interpreted as a punishment for infidelity to the covenant. Innocent people like Job do suffer, but they need not feel condemned by God. H. H. Rowley, a Scripture scholar, points out the immense significance of this message.

> By insisting that there is such a thing as innocent suffering, the author of Job is bringing a message of the first importance to the sufferer. The hardest part of his suffering need not be the feeling that he is deserted by God, or the fear that all men will regard him as cast out from God's presence. If his suffering is innocent it may not spell isolation from God, and when he most needs the sustaining presence of God he may still have it. Here is a religious message of great significance.[15]

The Book of Job is doubly significant for us. First, it challenges the dominant Old Testament meaning context approach. Second, it introduces into the Old Testament an entirely different approach to integrating suffering within a faith vision, an approach similar to the support context mindset. This approach rests not on discovering God's reasons for sending suffering but upon the experience of God's presence during suffering. While acknowledging that God is indeed causing his suffering, Job discovers the evidence of God's love not in these external events but in the intimacy of a heightened personal presence. Again Rowley:

> More significant is his recognition that, with all the loss and the pain he had suffered, he had gained something even from his agony. In his prosperity he thought he had known God. Now he realizes that compared with his former knowledge his present knowledge is as the joy of seeing compared with a mere rumor. All his past experience of God was as nothing compared with the experience he had now found. He therefore no longer cries out to God to be delivered from his suffering. He rests in God even in his pain.[16]

The Book of Job foreshadows the New Testament. Rowley points out that the message of Job is not far from the New Testament message as found in the epistles of Paul.

> "Concerning this thing I cried unto the Lord thrice, that it might depart from me. And He hath said unto me, my grace is sufficient for thee: for my power is made perfect in weakness. Most gladly therefore," cries Paul, "will I rather glory in my weaknesses, that the power of Christ may rest upon me" (2 Cor 12:8 ff.). Here we see that Paul

ceases to cry out for deliverance from his suffering, but finds enrichment in his suffering, so that he comes to rejoice in the suffering itself because it has brought him a new experience of the grace of God.
This is fundamentally the same as we have found in the book of Job.[17]

Two concluding notes. First, my use of the Old Testament has
been somewhat slanted. I have selected passages illustrating the meaning
context approach to suffering, the Jewish approach to suffering flowing
from God's control over creation and history as given in the covenant
stipulations. I have not selected passages illustrating the support context
approach to suffering, the Jewish experience of God's presence and power
during suffering. In no way, however, do I wish to imply that this experience is absent in the Old Testament. Throughout the Old Testament
God is presented as a Lord, steadfast and merciful, giving the Jews all
the strength needed, especially in suffering. The much loved Psalm 23
is but one example.

> The Lord is my shepherd;
> > there is nothing I lack.
> In green pastures you let me graze;
> > to safe waters you lead me;
> > you restore my strength.
> You guide me along the right path for the sake of your name.
> Even when I walk through a dark valley,
> > I fear no harm for you are at my side;
> > your rod and staff give me courage (Ps 23:1–4).

Also these verses from Isaiah's so-called Book of Consolation.

> Though young men faint and grow weary,
> > and youths stagger and fall,
> They that hope in the Lord will renew their strength,
> > they will soar as with eagles' wings;
> They will run and not grow weary,
> > walk and not grow faint (Is 40:30–31).

Second, I do not want to imply that the use of the meaning context
may not be helpful in the initial stages of coping with suffering. It is
significant that before reaching their final faith integration both Job and

Ivan Ilyich angrily challenged God with the perennial question, "Why me, O God?" One author notes that many psalms also begin in angry questioning of God's ways before concluding in praise. His observation on these "psalms of lament" is astute.

> A catharsis has taken place, almost as though the psalmist said, "I have had my chance to say my piece. Someone was willing to hear me out and not put down my pettiness and preoccupation with self and anger. I feel better now. I even recognize that some of the things I said were probably exaggerated and things aren't quite as bad as I have made them out to be. Now, if you have some word of encouragement for me, I may be able to hear it. I could not have heard it if you had forced it on me before I had time to get this off my chest."[18]

It is also significant that in Kübler-Ross' schema the stage of Anger precedes Acceptance. For religious people both stages involve God. But anger at God presumes faith. Perhaps anger is "cathartic" for many of us in dealing fully with suffering. No doubt God "can take it."

Yet the danger remains. Building faith upon the belief that God is the direct cause of suffering — for whatever reason — has potential for permanently alienating us from God. The man described earlier with three children to raise after the death of his wife had lost his wife some six years previously. He has been stuck on the level of anger all these years, with detrimental affects not only to his faith but also to his psychological and physical health. He had not attended to the message of Job.

### Meaning Context Approach: An Evaluation

We all need to make sense of life. This need is experienced most acutely when life involves suffering. The dominant Old Testament tradition gives one approach to reconciling God and suffering: God is the direct cause of suffering; God causes suffering for specific reasons. Since God is always just as well as loving, we can rest assured that whatever happens to us is 1) deserved and 2) a result of love. If we could understand God's purposes, we would gladly accept the suffering.

The logic is simple, but is it true? The Book of Job, while accepting the fact that God is the direct cause of all that happens, challenges the Jewish approach that misfortune is willed by God as punishment for

sin. Rabbi Kushner goes further. He not only denies the fact that suffering is a punishment for sin, but wonders whether God is the cause of
suffering for any of the reasons usually given.

> All the responses to tragedy which we have considered have at least
> one thing in common. They all assume that God is the cause of suf-
> fering, and they try to understand why God would want us to suffer.
> Is it for our own good, or is it a punishment we deserve, or could it
> be that God does not care what happens to us? . . . We were left
> either hating ourselves for deserving such a fate, or hating God for
> sending it to us when we did not deserve it.

> There may be another approach. Maybe God does not cause our suf-
> fering. Maybe it happens for some reason other than the will of God.
> The psalmist writes, "I lift mine eyes to the hills; from where does
> my help come? My help comes from the Lord, maker of Heaven and
> earth." (Psalm 121:1–2) He does not say, "My pain comes from the
> Lord," or "my tragedy comes from the Lord." He says "my *help* comes
> from the Lord."[19]

Kushner challenges Old Testament assumptions. From within a Jewish
context he moves away from the meaning context approach and toward
the support context. Though there are other aspects of his thought that
disturb me, in this we are in agreement.

And what of Carretto and the Christian use of the meaning context
approach? Recall that Carretto insists that God is the direct cause of
suffering, though he emphatically denies that God causes suffering as a
punishment for sin. He believes that God sends suffering to help us grow.
He witnesses to the great growth he experienced in coping with his
crippled leg. While fully agreeing with Carretto that suffering can be
crucial for growth, I disagree with him that God directly causes the suffering to accomplish this result.

But Carretto's approach has great appeal. Since all of us have grown
through suffering, it is tempting to assert that God sends suffering in
order to cause the growth. This approach offers immediate relief: God
knows best; God wants this to happen; I accept God's decision. But the
logic used is bad. We reason that *because* we have actually grown through
a suffering, *therefore* God must have sent the suffering for this purpose.
Such reasoning is flawed. Just because one event happens *after* another

doesn't necessarily mean it happened *because of* it.[20] Because we have grown through suffering doesn't necessarily mean God sent the suffering to give this growth.

The approach becomes increasingly troublesome when applied consistently to the vast amount of suffering in our world. It is difficult to maintain God's goodness. Does God cause all suffering? What of natural disasters — droughts, floods, hurricanes, earthquakes? What of social injustice — poverty, oppression? What of physical disease and handicaps — birth defects, cancer, AIDS? What of mental disease — compulsions, neuroses, psychoses? What of intentional human violence — war, genocide, murder, robbery, rape, incest? What of accidental human violence through carelessness — such as the deaths of our six students through careless driving of others? What of everyday accidents in life involving no intentional violence resulting in mental or physical handicaps or death — such as Carretto's? What of suffering occurring to those who cannot grow through it — the suffering of children? What of suffering that results not in growth but in diminishment and despair? And on and on.

I believe that focusing primarily on the meaning context approach in coping with suffering creates more problems than it solves. I also believe that it is not the dominant approach of the New Testament, though we can indeed detect its presence in certain texts. We now move to the New Testament and the support context approach.

## REFLECTION QUESTIONS

1. Do you interpret your sufferings as a punishment from God for your sins or your prosperity as a reward from God for your faithfulness? Explain.

2. Do you interpret major sufferings of our time as punishment from God for society's sins? Explain.

3. Do you agree with Carretto that God sends suffering to help us grow? Do you interpret any suffering in your life as sent by God for this purpose? Explain.

4. Do you interpret personal sufferings as sent by God to test your faith? Explain.

5. Have you ever experienced a special presence of God (like Job's) while challenging God over suffering? Explain.

6. Do you agree with the argument that because we frequently grow through suffering, therefore God sends suffering to help us grow?

# IV. STRENGTH IN SUFFERING: NEW TESTAMENT INSIGHTS

Jesus was a Jew, indeed, a very conscientious Jew. The New Testament reveals that he participated fully in the life of his people, observing Jewish feast days, praying daily at the three prescribed times, attending synagogue, frequenting the temple, calling his followers to the fullest observance of the Law and Prophets. But Jesus was a Jew with a unique perspective on being faithful to the covenant. As a wandering preacher, he spent much of his public life explaining his message to his followers and debating the meaning of the Scriptures with the scribes and Pharisees. Jesus shared with his fellow Jews the meaning of the Scriptures as revealed to him by God — whom he called *Father*! It is an understatement to assert that he disagreed with the official interpreters of Judaism in some very crucial areas. One of these areas of disagreement was God's relationship to suffering. John's Gospel presents Jesus in radical disagreement with the Pharisees' position that suffering, in this case blindness, is punishment for sin.

> As he passed by he [Jesus] saw a man blind from birth. His disciples asked him, "Rabbi, who sinned, this man or his parents, that he was born blind?" Jesus answered, "Neither this man nor his parents sinned; it is so that the works of God might be made visible through him" (Jn 9:1–4).

The blind man, healed by Jesus, was brought to the Pharisees. The Pharisees insisted Jesus must be a sinner because he had broken the Law by healing on the Sabbath — another area of disagreement. But no doubt about it, the man had been born blind — his parents concurred when summoned — and Jesus had cured him. The now-healed blind man challenges the Pharisees, denying that Jesus is a sinner and insisting Jesus must be from God: "If this man were not from God, he would not be able to do anything" (Jn 9:33). Relying on the Jewish tradition that blindness is a punishment for sin, the Pharisees gave the only retort left them, "You were born totally in sin, and are you trying to teach us?" (Jn 9:34). Jesus then removes the man's spiritual blindness as he asks for and receives faith in himself as the Son of Man. The scene concludes with a final denial by Jesus of the relationship between blindness and sin.

> Some of the Pharisees who were with him heard this and said to him, "Surely we are not also blind, are we?" Jesus said to them, "If you were blind, you would have no sin; but now you are saying, 'We see,' so your sin remains" (Jn 9:40–41).

John's account of the cure of the blind man gives the signal that the New Testament approach to suffering is different than the dominant Old Testament approach. New Testament narratives simply observe Jesus and his disciples facing suffering squarely with absolute confidence that God will give sufficient strength. Rather surprisingly in light of the dominant Old Testament tradition these texts present no systematic explanation for the presence of suffering. However, remnants of the meaning context approach can be detected, especially in the connection between suffering and sin found in some of the healing narratives — "Which is easier, to say to the paralytic, 'Your sins are forgiven,' or to say, 'Rise pick up your mat and walk'?" (Mk 2:9).

We now move from the meaning context approach to suffering to the support context approach. The Holy Spirit becomes again our focus. Since the New Testament presents both Jesus and Paul as living under the influence of the Spirit, our treatment highlights each as living within the Scriptural Model of the self described in Chapter II and handling suffering within this model.

### Jesus and the Spirit : Self-in-God

It is impossible to understand Jesus without understanding his roots in Judaism. Israel is distinct among all nations. The distinction relates to God's choice of Israel for the fullest revelation of God's self to the world. In Israel there is a privileged "intersection between the world of

the Spirit and the world of ordinary experience," as Marcus Borg writes.
Borg is helpful in appreciating the role of the Spirit in the Jewish tradition and as well as in Jesus himself, "The Hebrew Bible is Israel's story
of events which were seen as disclosures of Spirit, of people who were
experienced as mediators of Spirit, of law and prophetic utterance which
were believed to have been given by the Spirit."[1]

Individuals are chosen by God to be mediators of the Spirit. Foremost
among the Spirit-filled mediators of Israel are the prophets. Borg puts
Jesus with the group of charismatics called the prophets, "Of all the
figures in his tradition, Jesus was most like the classical prophets of
Israel."[2] Borg draws our attention to the fact that the New Testament
itself records that Jesus twice situated himself within this tradition.

> Not only did some of his contemporaries put him in the prophetic tra-
> dition, but he also twice referred to himself as one, albeit somewhat
> indirectly. In his home town he said, "a prophet is not without honor,
> except in his own country." Later, he said, "It cannot be that a prophet
> should perish away from Jerusalem." Identifying himself with the
> prophets, Jesus saw himself in the tradition of those who *knew* God.[3]

Similar to the prophets, Jesus was filled with the Spirit of God and so
*knew* God from personal experience. It was this experience of God that
gave these chosen mediators — and Jesus — the authority to speak on
behalf of God. They bridged two worlds — the world of the Spirit and
current culture.

> Thus the stream in which Jesus stood, going back through the prophets
> to the founder and fathers of Israel, as well as the stream which issued
> forth from him, centered on Spirit-filled mediators who bridged the
> two worlds. The stream was the source of the tradition; its literature,
> both the Hebrew Bible and the New Testament, clusters around them.
> Indeed, in the specific sense of the term used here, the heart of the
> biblical tradition is "charismatic," its origin lying in the experience
> of Spirit-endowed people who became radically open to the other
> world and whose gifts were extraordinary.[4]

It can be asked whether Jesus himself acknowledges that his
power came from the Spirit. The Gospels do not explicitly indicate this.
But since Jesus was aware of the role of the Spirit of God in the Old

Testament prophets, there is no reason to believe he would not be aware of a similar role of the Spirit in his own life. Most commentators would agree with Roger Haight's conclusion.

> What seems to be established is this: that Jesus experienced the power of God as Spirit in his life; that he was aware of this *in these terms;* that this empowerment was manifest in his actions; that these empowered actions were construed as the ruling of God; and that people recognized this even during his lifetime. (Italics mine.)[5]

Contemporary treatments of Jesus have not always respected the centrality of the Spirit in his life. But no adequate understanding of the historical Jesus is possible without recognizing Jesus' relationship to the Spirit. Cardinal Suenens of Belgium puts it succinctly.

> We must see the mystery of the Incarnation and the life of Jesus in the light of the central affirmation of the Credo: "He was born of the Virgin Mary by the Power of the Holy Spirit." To forget or minimize the role of the Holy Spirit is to deform the true countenance of the Lord and compromise his mission.[6]

Borg insists that the Spirit is the source of *all* Jesus' power in fulfilling his mission.

> The cumulative impression created by the synoptic gospels is very strong: Jesus stood in the charismatic tradition of Judaism which reached back to the beginnings of Israel. Matthew, Mark, and Luke all portray him as a Spirit-filled person through whom the power of the Spirit flowed. His relationship to Spirit was both the source and energy of the mission which he undertook.[7]

Borg continues, putting it starkly, "He [Jesus] is spiritual in that his relationship to the Spirit of God was the central reality in his life, the source of all that he was; we cannot glimpse the historical Jesus unless we take with utmost seriousness his relationship to the world of Spirit."[8]

These bold assertions are easy to substantiate by reading the Gospel of Luke with an eye for the Spirit passages. No passage is more significant than that concerning Jesus' conception. The angel's response to Mary's question reveals Jesus' unique relationship to the Spirit, "The holy Spirit will come upon you, and the power of the Most High will overshadow you. Therefore the child to be born will be called holy, the Son of God" (Lk 1:35). The Spirit becomes the paternal factor in the conception of Jesus.

Also central is the account of the opening of Jesus' public ministry. The fact that the account appears in all four Gospels indicates its historical origins in Jesus' life as well as its significance in the faith of the early Church. Jesus was among the crowd at the Jordan River listening to the preaching of John the Baptist. In prayer after he had been baptized a startling event occurred. "After all the people had been baptized and Jesus had been baptized and was praying, heaven was opened and the holy Spirit descended upon him in bodily form like a dove. And a voice came from heaven, 'You are my beloved Son; with you I am well pleased'" (Lk 3:21–22). And so all Jesus' subsequent activity is put in the context of approval by the Father and empowerment by the Spirit.

References to the Spirit continue in Luke's Gospel. After John's baptism Jesus goes to the desert. "Filled with the holy Spirit, Jesus returned from the Jordan and was led by the Spirit into the desert for forty days, to be tempted by the devil" (Lk 4:1–2). Then after the desert experience Jesus initiates his public ministry not in Jerusalem but up north in Galilee. "Jesus returned to Galilee in the power of the Spirit, and news of him spread throughout the whole region. He taught in their synagogues and was praised by all" (Lk 4:14–15). And soon after his arrival Jesus goes to his hometown synagogue at Nazareth, unrolls the scroll of Isaiah and reads a passage referring to an anointing by God with the Spirit.

> "The Spirit of the Lord is upon me,
>     because he has anointed me to bring glad tidings to the poor.
> He has sent me to proclaim liberty to captives
>     and recovery of sight to the blind, to let the oppressed go free,
> and to proclaim a year acceptable to the Lord."
>
> Rolling up the scroll, he handed it back to the attendant and sat down, and the eyes of all in the synagogue looked intently at him. He said to them, "Today this scripture is fulfilled in your hearing" (Lk 4:18–21).

Thus in the Gospel of Luke does Jesus place himself among the Spirit-filled mediators of the Old Testament.

The accounts of the transfiguration are also significant. The Gospels of Matthew, Mark and Luke all put Jesus on a level with two key Spirit-endowed figures of Jewish Scriptures, Moses and Elijah. So close is the association that Peter suggests that three tents be erected, one each for Jesus, Moses and Elijah. In this way all the Synoptic Gospels present Jesus as having the same connection with the world of the Spirit as Moses and Elijah. The voice from the cloud further confirms the appropriateness of putting Jesus on the same level with these mediators, "This is my chosen Son; listen to him" (Lk 9:35). The voice also recalls the baptism account with the voice from the Father and the appearance of the Dove-Spirit.

The New Testament presents Jesus as called to live his life, as we are called to live ours, in response to God's Spirit. Of course we must acknowledge that Jesus' relationship to God is unique because of his unique relationship to God through the hypostatic union, yet we can truly affirm that the Gospels present Jesus as living within the Scriptural Model of the self as described in Chapter II. Thus Jesus becomes for Christians the example *par excellence* of response to the Spirit –– an example to be imitated in all life and especially in suffering. The crucial question for our university community after the automobile accidents was not as we supposed "Why are You doing this to us, O God?" but rather "What can we learn from Jesus for handling our suffering?"

## Jesus and Suffering: Support Context

Jesus suffered. To many this is self-evident; to others it's not. I believe it is self-evident because Jesus has a human nature and suffering is part of the human condition. The teaching of the Christian Church was formalized by the Council of Chalcedon in 451 with its declaration that Jesus, while remaining a single person, was truly divine, like the Father in his divinity, and truly human, like us in his humanity. How these two dimensions of Jesus are related has never been defined by the Church and will always remain a mystery. But we cannot remain orthodox Christians in harmony with the Ecumenical Councils of the early Church without maintaining both.

Unfortunately many of the presentations of Jesus in the past have so stressed the divinity that they have by implication denied the humanity. These approaches undervalued the reality of Jesus' full participation in the human condition preferring to focus on Jesus as the Incarnate Word of God living temporarily on earth. Recent scholarship is attempting to restore the balance by paying special attention to Jesus' humanity. It has been helped by the teaching of Vatican II. The Church is insisting anew on the importance of maintaining the full humanity of Jesus. Only because our human nature has been fully assumed by Jesus has it has been transformed to a divine dignity. And because Jesus has fully assumed it he is truly one of us. Vatican Council II puts it well.

> Since human nature as He assumed it was not annulled, by that very fact it has been raised up to a divine dignity in our respect too. For by His Incarnation the Son of God has united Himself in some fashion with every man. He worked with human hands, He thought with a human mind, acted by human choice, and loved with a human heart. Born of the Virgin Mary, He has truly been made one of us, like us in all things except sin.[9]

The assertion that Jesus is "one of us, like us in all things except sin" is from the Epistle to the Hebrews. This epistle insists that even though Jesus is a great high priest he can remain compassionate because he is also one of us. "For we do not have a high priest who is unable to sympathize with our weaknesses, but one who has similarly been tested in every way, yet without sin" (Heb 4:15). Since he fully shares our human condition he can be a model for living our lives and therefore a model for handling our suffering.

Though we are concerned primarily with how Jesus handled his own suffering a brief note on Jesus' approach to the suffering of others is in order. The Gospels are clear, abounding with healing stories: Jesus' heart was always moved with pity by suffering and he always did what he could to relieve it. He taught his disciples to do the same, insisting that serving others was central to being his disciple. "I was hungry and you gave me to eat, thirsty and you gave me to drink."

What were Jesus' sufferings? Too often our understanding of Jesus' suffering focuses only on his final suffering and only on one dimension, the physical pain. But it is important to appreciate that as a full partaker in the human condition Jesus' daily suffering was not unlike our own. Jesus' life contained suffering, and at every level — physical, psychological and spiritual. Indeed with a heart acutely in tune with itself and with others, Jesus' daily sufferings must have been immense. Their sources are limitless and perhaps not usually fully appreciated: a sense of failure and frustration because of his inability to convince the people of his message from the Father; loneliness (rejection, even betrayal and denial) from not being understood by those he chose as intimates; sadness with the poor and outcast of his society because of their pitiable condition. Insights into Jesus' empathetic suffering emerge throughout the Gospels: the Beatitudes with their predilection for the poor, hungry, sorrowful; the observation preceding many healings that his heart was moved with pity; the lament over Jerusalem whose people he would gather to himself as a mother hen does her chickens — even as Jerusalem was rejecting him.

And after all this, his final suffering. Though the physical pain of the passion and crucifixion was intense, the mental and spiritual anguish was even more so. The blood and tears of the agony in Gethsemane as well as the cry of abandonment on Calvary give privileged insight into his spiritual suffering.

How did Jesus deal with his own suffering? We must admit that the Gospels present Jesus as spending very little time explicitly dealing with the *theoretical problem* of God's relationship to suffering that so dominated the Old Testament, the "Why, O God?" question. As we have indicated there is no systematic response given to the question anywhere in the New Testament. The Gospels do, however, show that Jesus did on occasion explicitly reject the Old Testament approach. The healing of the blind man in the Gospel of John is an explicit denial of this approach, even as the Pharisees were asserting it. Perhaps an even more eloquent repudiation are the Beatitudes themselves. Jesus actually turns upside down the conventional wisdom of the day — Blessed are you poor; woe to you who are rich!

> Blessed are you who are poor, for the kingdom of God is yours.
> Blessed are you who are now hungry, for you will be satisfied.
> Blessed are you who are now weeping, for you will laugh (Lk 6:20–21).

> But woe to you who are rich, for you have received your consolation.
> But woe to you who are filled now, for you will be hungry.
> But woe to you who laugh now, for you will grieve and weep
> (Lk 6:24–25).

It is difficult for us to appreciate the radicalness of the Beatitudes to Jesus' Jewish contemporaries. Indeed it is the repudiation of this fundamental Jewish conviction that Borg believes is at the heart of Jesus' Spirit-inspired message for his people.

> Jewish conventional wisdom . . . saw reality as organized on the basis of rewards and punishments. Reality was "built" that way. Living the way of wisdom, the path of righteousness, brought blessing; following the way of folly or wickedness brought ruin and death. . . . Most also believed that the path of conventional wisdom produced rewards in this world. The righteous would flourish and be blessed with children, a good name, possessions, and a long life.[10]

Jesus rejected this view. His message was good news to the poor because it was the poor whose situation kept them from fulfilling the prescripts of the Torah and so living among the people the culture deemed as "just."

> At the very least, Jesus challenged the connection between righteousness and prosperity made by conventional wisdom, with its corollary that the poor had not lived right and thus were "unworthy" children of Abraham. Moreover, because the standards of culture are internalized even in those who fail to meet those standards, the poor would have seen *themselves* as "unworthy" children of Abraham. Indeed, most of the poor were among the nonobservant. By accepting "the poor," Jesus as one in touch with the Spirit of God would have enabled the poor to see themselves differently.[11]

Though a theoretical solution to the problem of suffering is lacking in the Gospels, a *practical solution* is not. In practice Jesus handled suffering the same way he handled all the aspects of his life: trusting in the Father. It is that simple. The Gospels present Jesus as the definitive Spirit-filled mediator, the Messiah of God who received the fullness of the Spirit to discharge his mission. And the Gospels present Jesus as continually seeking the Father's guidance and strength to perform the mission. Jesus' withdrawal to Mount Tabor before setting his face for Jerusalem and his retreat to Gethsemane before his arrest and crucifixion reflect a lifelong rhythm of turning to the Father for strength and guidance — especially during his trials.

An insight into Jesus' attitude to the Father can be gleaned from the prayer Jesus taught his disciples, the Lord's Prayer. When asked how they should pray, Jesus simply shared his prayer, his attitudes. He taught them first to address God with the same familiarity and intimacy as he did, as "Abba," "Father." And then he taught them to pray for the same desire to serve this Father that dominated his own life: "Thy kingdom come, Thy will be done." And finally he taught them to pray for the same confidence in his Father as he had for all his material and spiritual needs: "Give us this day our daily bread." A student of mine gave me an insight into the significance of the word *abba* for Jews. While praying amid crowds of people at the Temple Wall in Jerusalem, the Wailing Wall, she observed a lost child panic and begin screaming "Abba," "Abba"; then she saw a young man emerge from the crowd and sweep the boy to his breast, holding him there until he stopped crying.

No passage in the Gospels witnesses more directly to Jesus' trust in the Father than the prayer in Gethsemane. It is also the best witness to the role of the Spirit in strengthening and guiding Jesus during suffering. Since this scene occurs in the gospels of Matthew, Mark and Luke many scholars believe it represents an actual historical occurrence. Though the Gospels present Jesus as frequently withdrawing from the crowds to be with the Father in prayer, only in this passage do we have the very words revealing how he himself approached his Father in his own suffering.

> Then going out he went, as was his custom, to the Mount of Olives, and the disciples followed him. When he arrived at the place he said to them, "Pray that you may not undergo the test." After withdrawing about a stone's throw from them and kneeling, he prayed, saying, "Father, if you are willing, take this cup away from me; still, not my will but yours be done." And to strengthen him an angel from heaven appeared to him. He was in such agony and he prayed so fervently that his sweat became like drops of blood falling on the ground (Lk 22:39–44).

Again Jesus' use of the Aramaic *Abba* for *Father* is central to grasping Jesus' relationship to the Father. It connotes the same loving intimacy and trust that characterizes the relationship of a small child to a father.

The phrase "as was his custom" implies further that this withdrawal to the Mount of Olives was a regular pattern for Jesus. It's easy to imagine Jesus' withdrawing regularly to the solitude of this secluded place outside the walls of the city especially during times of stress. The phrase "not my will but yours be done" reminds us that he saw his entire life as fulfilling his mission as God's prophet. And the reference to the "agony" and to "sweat like drops of blood" highlights his acute mental and spiritual suffering. But the mention of an "angel from heaven" sent "to strengthen him" indicates God answered his prayer and comforted him with a renewed experience of presence. In the Bible angels are frequently the messengers of God; often they fulfill the same role as the Spirit of God. In the Gospel of Luke God's angel strengthens Jesus; in Matthew and Mark Jesus' strength is restored through prayer but there is no mention of an angel.

Yet the depth of suffering was yet to come. On the cross itself Jesus experienced a level of suffering that was unrelieved by any comforting angel and cried out from Psalm 22, "My God, my God, why have you abandoned me?" (Mk 15:34). Jesus enters a level of human suffering — spiritual suffering — so intense he felt abandoned by his Father. He had already been rejected by the Jews, deserted by his followers and even denied and betrayed by two specially chosen disciples. His only support was his Father. Now it seemed even his Father had forsaken him. Raymond Brown insists we cannot explain away this scandalous cry from the cross.

> Those who exalt the divinity of Jesus to the point where they cannot allow him to be truly human interpret away this verse to fit their christology. They insist that Psalm 22 ends with God delivering the suffering figure. That may well be, but the verse that Jesus is portrayed as quoting is not the verse of deliverance but the verse of abandonment — a verse by a suffering psalmist who is puzzled because up to now God has always supported and heard him. It is an exaggeration to speak of Jesus' despair, for he still speaks to *"my* God." Yet Matthew, following Mark, does not hesitate to show Jesus in the utter agony of feeling forsaken as he faces a terrible death. We are not far here from the christology of Hebrews which portrays Jesus as experiencing the whole human condition, like us in everything but sin.[12]

But the Father is there. In Gethsemane the Father is there as a comforting presence strengthening Jesus; on Calvary the Father is there sustaining Jesus' faith; there is no despair. Jesus' last words from the cross in the Gospel of Luke sum up the childlike trust of a lifetime, "Father, into your hands I commend my spirit" (Lk 23:6). As Jesus had trusted the Father in life, so he now trusts the Father in death.

The Gospel is clear: Jesus experienced human suffering and Jesus relied on his Father for help. Jesus exemplifies the support context approach to suffering. The support context approach to suffering presented in Chapter I is based upon the convictions that 1) God gives strength for our lives and 2) God gives strength in suffering. To be faithful to the witness of Jesus in the Gospel the support context approach should be expanded (recall that our original description was intended for all religions): 1) **through the Spirit Jesus receives strength from the Father to fulfill his mission; 2) through the Spirit Jesus receives strength for his suffering; 3) through the Spirit Jesus is transformed by his suffering.**

Only the third may need further explanation — or it may not. The Father raised Jesus from the dead, transforming Jesus' physical body into a spiritual one. The ancient Nicene Creed expresses the central conviction of all Christians: "On the third day he rose again in accordance with the scriptures; he ascended into heaven and is seated at the right hand of the Father." An ancient liturgical hymn found in Paul reflects the connection between Jesus' obedient suffering and his exaltation. Paul is exhorting his readers to adopt this same attitude in their own suffering.

> Who, though he was in the form of God,
> did not regard equality with God something to be grasped.
> Rather, he emptied himself, taking the form of a slave,
> coming in human likeness; and found in human appearance,
> he humbled himself, becoming obedient to death, even death on a cross.
> Because of this, God greatly exalted him
> and bestowed on him a name that is above every name,
> that at the name of Jesus every knee should bend,
> of those in heaven, on earth and under the earth,
> and every tongue confess that Jesus Christ is Lord,
> to the glory of God the Father (Phil 2:7–11).

*Gospel* means "good news." For Christians the good news is two-fold: Christ's resurrection from the dead is the pledge of our own and the power that sustained Christ in his life sustains us in ours — at Pentecost Christ and the Father send the Spirit. What can we learn from Jesus for handling the suffering of the automobile accidents? Trust in the Father's love; it is sufficient for every need; it can even transform us through our suffering. No one in the New Testament gives better witness to this power and trust than Paul.

### Paul and the Spirit: Self-in-God

Paul's faith in Jesus began with his dramatic encounter with the resurrected Christ on the road to Damascus. Significantly Paul's conversion to Christ occurred neither as a consequence of scholarly reflection on Jesus as fulfillment of the prophecies, nor as a result of early Christian preaching, nor even because of the courageous witness of the first disciples whom he was actively persecuting — Acts 8 tells us he thoroughly approved of the killing of Stephen. The change in Paul occurred through an experience of Jesus, "Now I want you to know, brothers, that the gospel preached by me is not of human origin. For I did not receive it from a human being, nor was I taught it, but it came through a revelation of Jesus Christ" (Gal 1:11–12). At Damascus Paul received his mission from God: preach the Gospel to the Gentiles.

And this encounter with Jesus gave Paul the power to accomplish this mission. His letters witness to this power in his life as well as in the communities he served, "I am not ashamed of the gospel. It is the power of God leading everyone who believes in it to salvation, the Jew first, then the Greek" (Rom 1:16). Our focus is on Paul's personal experience of this power. Thomas Tobin sees the notion of power as the central metaphor for Paul's approach to life.

> All of us have basic strategies for dealing with ourselves and with the world around us. . . . These basic strategies influence all of our particular viewpoints and decisions. Put another way, each of us is guided by root paradigms or root metaphors. . . . The same was true for Paul. In his case those root metaphors or paradigms clustered around the notion of power. Both before and after his call or conversion, Paul's images of God and of Christ were deeply influenced by those images of power.[13]

An appreciation of the dimensions of this power is key for understanding Paul personally and consequently for understanding his message, especially his insistence on justification by faith — as opposed to justification by observance of the Mosaic Law — bringing with it a new freedom from the Law, sin, death, suffering.

Paul's references to God's power, often combined with God's wisdom, frequently present the Spirit as their source. And Paul regularly contrasts this power with human weakness.

> When I came to you, brethren, I did not come proclaiming to you the testimony of God in lofty words or wisdom. For I decided to know nothing among you except Jesus Christ and him crucified. And I was with you in weakness and in much fear and trembling; and my speech and my message were not in plausible words of wisdom, but in the demonstration of the Spirit and power, that your faith might not rest in the wisdom of men but in the power of God (1 Cor 2:1–5 from Revised Standard Version).

The power and wisdom of Christ contrast with both Jewish and Greek claims.

> For the Jews demand signs and Greeks look for wisdom, but we proclaim Christ crucified, a stumbling block to Jews and foolishness to Gentiles, but to those who are called, Jews and Greeks alike, Christ the power of God and the wisdom of God. For the foolishness of God is wiser than human wisdom, and the weakness of God is stronger than human strength (1 Cor 1:22–25).

Recall that Paul often contrasts his life "in Christ" with his life as an observant Pharisee before the Damascus event. Paul's letters emphasize three key manifestations of God's power flowing from the Spirit: freedom from the Mosaic law, from slavery to sin, from fear of death. The Spirit freed him from subservience to the Mosaic law; he need now live in response to the inner law of the Spirit written in his heart. Paul's annoyance at the Galatians for not trusting this power is forthright.

> O stupid Galatians! Who has bewitched you, before whose eyes Jesus Christ was publicly crucified? I want to learn only this from you: did

you receive the Spirit from the works of the law, or from faith in what you heard? Are you so stupid? After beginning with the Spirit, are you now ending with the flesh? Did you experience so many things in vain? — if indeed it was in vain. Does, then, the one who supplies the Spirit to you and works mighty deeds among you do so from works of the law or from faith in what you heard? (Gal 3:1–6).

The Spirit also freed him from moral weakness, from slavery to the sinful demands of his body, his flesh. Though temptations remain the power of the Spirit is sufficient for dealing with them.

I say, then: live by the Spirit and you will certainly not gratify the desire of the flesh. For the flesh has desires against the Spirit, and the Spirit against the flesh; these are opposed to each other, so that you may not do what you want. . . . Now the works of the flesh are obvious: immorality, impurity, licentiousness, idolatry, sorcery, hatreds, rivalry, jealousy. . . . In contrast, the fruit of the Spirit is love, joy, peace, patience, kindness, generosity, faithfulness, gentleness, self-control. . . . If we live in the Spirit, let us also follow the Spirit (Gal 5:16–25, passim).

Finally the Spirit freed him from fear of death. Since the Spirit constitutes all believers as children of God, believers are co-heirs with Christ of heaven. Jesus' resurrection is the pledge of our resurrection — we need not fear death.

For those who are led by the Spirit of God are children of God. For you did not receive a spirit of slavery to fall back unto fear; but you received a spirit of adoption, through which we cry, *Abba,* "Father!" The Spirit itself bears witness with our spirit that we are children of God, and if children, then heirs, heirs of God and joint heirs with Christ, if only we suffer with him so that we may also be glorified with him (Rom 8:14–17).

The passage is also important for revealing the connection in Paul's mind between suffering and glorification — for Christ as well as for ourselves.

Through faith in Jesus, Paul received a new power of the Spirit transforming every aspect of his life and giving him strength to fulfill his mission from God. This power of God was also central in dealing with suffering. Paul's epistles indicate that after the Damascus event he understood his life within the Scriptural Model of the self, fully aware of the centrality of the Spirit. And his epistles witness that he like Christ handled his suffering within the support context approach.

## Paul and Suffering: Support Context

Paul's ministry occasioned much personal suffering. Throughout his letters he makes references to them.[14] Tradition says that he was eventually martyred in Rome in the persecution of Nero after trials and imprisonment first in Palestine and then in Rome. How did Paul handle his sufferings? It is not surprising to discover that Paul handled his suffering the same way he handled all the areas of his life: trusting in the power of God. What is surprising is discovering that nowhere in the epistles does Paul engage in a theoretical discussion on the reasons for suffering. As a devout Jew, Paul was thoroughly familiar with the Jewish convictions that God rewarded and punished believers in accordance with their fidelity to the covenant. Since Paul's life contained so much personal suffering it is indeed surprising he never wrestled formally with Job's questions.

To put his epistles in context we must recall his belief that the end of the world was imminent and that much of the suffering Christians were experiencing were signs of the final struggle between God and God's enemies — Satan being the foremost. Since Christians were being persecuted at this time his letters were intended to give hope during these persecutions. Paul wished to assure them that the power of Christ was stronger than the power of Satan and they could be confident of victory in this final cosmic struggle. Christ's resurrection is the pledge of their eventual victory.

> But now Christ has been raised from the dead, the firstfruits of those who have fallen asleep. For since death came through a human being, the resurrection of the dead came also through a human being. For just as in Adam all die, so too in Christ shall all be brought to life, but each one in proper order: Christ the firstfruits; then, at his coming, those who belong to Christ; then comes the end, when he hands over the kingdom to his God and Father, when he has destroyed

every sovereignty and every authority and power. For he must reign until he has put all his enemies under his feet. The last enemy to be destroyed is death (1 Cor 15:20–27).

But our primary concern is Paul's approach to the suffering connected with his mission of preaching the Gospel to the Gentiles. What are Paul's attitudes toward these sufferings? Tobin notes three specific attitudes emerging in Paul's epistles giving key insights into how Paul was able to integrate his sufferings within his faith vision.[15] First, sufferings aid his ministry because they witness to his sincerity.

> We put no obstacle in any one's way, so that no fault may be found with our ministry. But as servant of God we commend ourselves in every way: through great endurance, in affliction, hardships, calamities, beatings, imprisonments, tumults, labors, watching, hunger; by purity, knowledge, forbearance, kindness, holiness of spirit, genuine love, truthful speech, and the power of God (2 Cor 6:3–6 from Revised Standard Version).

Second, suffering enhances conformity to Christ, for himself and for his communities.

> But we hold this treasure in earthen vessels, that the surpassing power may be of God and not from us. We are afflicted in every way, but not constrained; perplexed, but not driven to despair; persecuted, but not abandoned; struck down, but not destroyed; always carrying about in the body the dying of Jesus, so that the life of Jesus may also be manifested in our body. For we are constantly being given up to death for the sake of Jesus, so that the life of Jesus may be manifested in our mortal flesh (2 Cor 4:7–11).

Third, suffering leads to personal growth because of our confidence in the power of the Spirit to sustain us no matter what happens.

> Not only that, but we even boast in our afflictions, knowing that affliction produces endurance, and endurance, proven character, and proven character, hope, and hope does not disappoint, because the love of God has been poured our into our hearts through the holy Spirit that has been given us (Rom 5:3–5).

For Paul suffering occasioned by his mission can be integrated within his faith vision: it enhances effectiveness as an apostle, fosters conformity with Christ and produces continual transformation of character with assurances of final glory.

No chapters in the epistles give more insight into Paul's approach to handling personal suffering than 2 Corinthians 10–13. Paul's right to minister has come under attack. To defend himself he employs an ingenious method. He claims that his accusers "write their own references"; but Paul insists that his references for ministry are from God. He then boasts how abundant are his own references from God, using several different approaches. Paul boasts that he has been given the authority to preach directly from Christ himself — recall the Damascus account; he boasts that he has been steadfastly faithful to this commission from Christ and has been so without imposing the burden of supporting him on others; he boasts that God has in addition benefited him with extraordinary visions and revelations.

Finally, Paul decides to defend his ministry by boasting about the sufferings he has endured. Paul is again comparing himself to his accusers. He asserts he has worked harder, been imprisoned and beaten more than any of them. He continues boasting in his sufferings.

> Five times I had thirty-nine lashes from the Jews; three time I have been beaten with sticks; once I was stoned; three times I have been shipwrecked and once adrift in the open sea a night and a day. Constantly traveling, I have been in danger from rivers and in danger from brigands, in danger from my own people and in danger from pagans; in danger in the towns, in danger in the open country, in danger at sea and in danger from so-called brothers. I have worked and labored, often without sleep; I have been hungry and thirsty and often starving; I have been in the cold without clothes (2 Cor 11:25–28).

And how does Paul handle these sufferings? Paul makes direct reference to a particularly bothersome on-going suffering, the famous "thorn in the flesh" (whose meaning remains a mystery).[16] The conclusion of the passage, however, implies that his other sufferings are handled similarly — all his weaknesses, insults, hardships, persecutions and agonies. There is no more graphic witness to God's power in human weakness in all Paul's writings. I believe the following passage is the closest we get in all Paul's letters to his own method of handling suffering.

> In view of the extraordinary nature of these revelations, to stop me
> from getting too proud I was given a thorn in the flesh, an angel of
> Satan to beat me and stop me from getting too proud! About this thing,
> I have pleaded with the Lord three times for it to leave me, but he has
> said, "My grace is enough for you: my power is at its best in weak-
> ness." So I shall be very happy to make my weakness my special boast
> so that the power of Christ may stay over me, and that is why I am
> quite content with my weaknesses, and with insults, hardships, per-
> secutions, and the agonies I go through for Christ's sake. For it is
> when I am weak that I am strong (2 Cor 12:7–10).

Paul's struggle with his thorn in the flesh, begging three times that
it be removed, is reminiscent of Jesus' own struggle in Gethsemane.
God's response to Paul's prayer is also reminiscent: "My grace is enough
for you." Paul was indeed imitating Jesus in dealing with his suffering
by acknowledging his need, seeking strength from God and then continuing his service to God trusting the power of God given him. It should
be noted that Paul does impute to God a reason for this particular suffering: "to stop me from being too proud." The intent of the passage,
however, remains the same: in human weakness God's power is most
fully manifest. Victor Furnish observes a significant contrast between
Paul's approach to suffering and typical approaches of the day.

> Paul therefore does not, like the Cynic and Stoic philosophers of his
> day, strive to transcend his weaknesses by dismissing them as trifling.
> Nor does he, like them, hold to the ideal of self-sufficiency, striving
> to limit his needs and therefore his dependency on others. Rather,
> precisely by accepting his tribulations as real weaknesses he is led
> by them to acknowledge his ultimate dependence on God. Thereby
> his weaknesses — not just the frailty which inevitably characterizes
> his creaturely status, but the adversities and afflictions he has had to
> bear as an apostle — have become a means by which the incompa-
> rable power of God is revealed.[17]

What can we learn from Paul for dealing with suffering? Clearly
Paul, like Christ, lives within the Scriptural Model of the self and deals
with suffering through the support context mindset. But Paul is different from Christ in one important way: he receives help in suffering not

only through his relationship with the Father but also through his relationship with Christ. Consequently our support context paradigm must be adjusted slightly to include this double relationship.

The following expansion of the diagram applies to Paul — and to all Christians. The "strength to love" in the diagram refers to strength received to be faithful both to our common baptismal vocations as well as to our individual vocations of service to others. "Suffering" includes any obstacle — internal weakness or external adversities — to living the Gospel. Please note that in the support context approach suffering is integrated within the faith vision not by insights into God's reasons — these remain unknown — but by assurances of God's strength.

Only the final statement of the diagram needs further comment. Paul's epistles clearly assert that the Spirit gives strength for living the Gospel not only in good times but most especially in troubled times. But they assert even more. Precisely through our sufferings the Spirit conforms us more fully to Christ *who also suffered.* Evidences of the importance of suffering in Paul's transformation appear in most of the passages quoted above, and they abound in his epistles, "I have been crucified with Christ; yet I live, no longer I, but Christ lives in me" (Gal 2:19–20).

### Diagram 4
### New Testament Approach to Suffering

**Support Context:**
**Help me, O Lord!**

Perceived
Disorder:
Faith-Threatening

1. Through the Spirit we
   receive strength to love
   from the Father and Jesus
2. Through the Spirit we
   receive strength to love
   especially in suffering
3. Through suffering we are
   conformed more fully to
   Christ in loving and
   serving others

Perceived
Order:
Faith-Integrated

This conformity with Christ in suffering is given to Christians not only for our own personal comfort but also for the sake of strengthening us to love and serve others even during suffering.

## Support Context Approach: An Evaluation

Where is God in suffering? The typical Jew of Paul's day might presume that God — or Satan, with God's consent — is causing suffering as a punishment for infidelity to the covenant. Yet nowhere does Paul ever suggest that his own suffering is sent by God as a punishment for sin. Indeed it would not even strike us as surprising should Paul, like Job, be at least a little disturbed by the extent of his trials.

Rather than complain to God about his sufferings, Paul boasts in them — something unheard of in the Jewish tradition. Far from alienating him from God, Paul's trials have become privileged occasions for experiencing God's power. Paul has nothing to fear either from his own personal weaknesses or from external persecution from others; he has it directly from the Lord that God's power is sufficient for dealing with any trial. There is no more direct expression of this confidence than his letter to the Church in Rome, a Church that was undergoing persecution for faith.

> Who will separate us from the love of Christ? Trial, or distress, or persecution, or hunger, or nakedness, or danger, or the sword? As Scripture says: "For your sake we are being slain all the day long: we are looked upon as sheep to be slaughtered." Yet in all this we are more than conquerors because of him who has loved us. For I am certain that neither death nor life, neither angels nor principalities, neither the present nor the future, nor powers, neither height nor depth nor any other creature, will be able to separate us from the love of God that comes to us in Christ Jesus our Lord (Rom 8:35–39).

In this Paul is simply following his master Jesus. God had called Jesus and Paul to service of the kingdom. God gave both a full measure of the Spirit to perform his mission. And God transformed each through suffering. The power of God evident throughout their ministry is manifested most dramatically in their suffering. For Jesus and Paul, suffering becomes a way of knowing God's presence and love — one hesitates to say — even more intimately. And what reasons for suffering are given?

Reasons are not demanded by Jesus or Paul nor are they given by God. Perhaps Paul's exclamation in Romans is the best expression of his mind.

> Oh, the depth of the riches and wisdom and knowledge of God! How inscrutable are his judgments and how unsearchable his ways! "For who has known the mind of the Lord or who has been his counselor?" (Rom 11:33–34).

## REFLECTION QUESTIONS

1. Do you believe that Jesus truly suffered? What do you see as his greatest suffering? Explain.

2. Does any situation in your life lead you to identify with Jesus in Gethsemane, that is, going to God in extreme suffering and experiencing a comforting angel? Explain.

3. Does any situation in your life lead you to identify with Jesus in his expression of abandonment on the cross, that is, going to God in extreme suffering and receiving only the grace to "hang on" in faith? Explain.

4. What are your daily sufferings, "thorns in the flesh"? Have any of them been regular occasions for experiencing special strength from God? Explain.

5. Do you agree that Jesus and Paul approached suffering within the support context mindset? How does this compare with your typical approach? Explain.

6. In which personal sufferings — past or present — do you recognize the power of the Spirit most at work in your life? Explain.

# V. SUFFERING WITH CHRIST: HOW JESUS SAVES US

Regularly I open my course on Christology with a simple question: "How does Jesus save us?" Most of the students are relieved when they are able to recall the lessons of their early religious training: "Jesus saves us from original sin by dying on the cross and opening the gates of heaven." Most of the class is able to recall the story of the first sin. Adam and Eve disobeyed God and were driven from paradise. Humanity was now permanently estranged from God; the gates of heaven were closed. But God so loved us that God sent Jesus, God's own son, to redeem us. Since Jesus was truly human, he was able to represent us before God. Since he was also truly divine, he was able to atone for the offense against the divinity. And so by dying on the cross Jesus redeemed us from sin. I push the students, "Granted that Jesus' death opens the gates of heaven for us when we die, does his death and resurrection make any difference in our lives before we die?" Most are not sure.

Explaining that there are no right or wrong answers — only honest and dishonest — I venture to ask, "Do you have a relationship with Jesus?" Most have not given the matter any thought. Many reply that they have a relationship with God but not with Jesus, adding "Since Jesus and God are one, what difference does it make?" Eventually two types of relationships with Jesus emerge. For some Jesus is a friend. They pray to Jesus and have experienced the presence of Jesus. They are comfortable to varying degrees calling Jesus "friend." For others, the majority, Jesus is a model for imitation. A relationship exists in that Jesus' teaching and example have become, again to varying degrees, their ideals for life. But I don't think it is an exaggeration to say that for most students Christ plays a rather insignificant role in their faith. I've discovered that my students are not untypical Christians; many of us relate to God almost as if Christ is irrelevant.

But most of us are in touch to some degree with the power of God in our life, especially in dealing with suffering. I ask the students to recall the major sufferings of their past life and to ask whether their faith made any difference in the handling of these sufferings. Most have had major sufferings; most can even recall times when their faith has helped them. Often the suffering involves illnesses or deaths of loved ones — especially grandparents and high school friends — or troubled family situations often ending in divorce. They are aware of receiving strength from God and of being comforted by the Christian belief in an afterlife. I then ask students to recall ordinary daily sufferings and ask whether their faith makes any difference in handling them. Most students acknowledge that they do in fact pray, going to God in times of stress over relationships, grades, careers. Many acknowledge that these prayers make a difference in handling their stress.

For many the transition from the topic of suffering to that of redemption is awkward: "What does experiencing strength in suffering have to do with redemption? Isn't redemption about sin?" Surely, but more than sin. I believe we are talking about redemption whenever we are talking about the power of the Holy Spirit — the Spirit sent by Jesus and the Father after the Resurrection. We've seen Paul's witness to various dimensions of this power; the Spirit not only frees Paul from domination by his sinful inclinations but also gives Paul strength to deal with his sufferings. We can affirm that books on suffering are not only books about *spirituality* — as we did in Chapter II — but also books about *redemption* because they explore the significance of Christ's life and death for "saving us" from being overwhelmed by life's trials. Sadly many Christians have relegated redemption to something happening two thousand years ago but having no real effect on present life.

This chapter situates our treatment of suffering within an understanding of redemption; it focuses on Christ. Topics treated include reviewing the relationship between Christ and the Spirit in redemption, establishing a relationship with Jesus, living this relationship in suffering, and examining the meaning of "the Cross" in Christian life. We want to apply the New Testament insights to our own daily lives. Our discussion presumes an acceptance of the Scriptural Model of the self and of the support context mindset for dealing with suffering.

But we cannot examine the relevance of the New Testament for handling our sufferings until we name them. It will be helpful to review the overview given in Chapter I. Recall the three levels of suffering: physiological, psychological, spiritual. What are my primary sufferings at each level? What is my greatest suffering now? Are there any sufferings I am afraid to face? Dealing with suffering fully demands using all resources available to us. Without undervaluing the physiological and psychological resources, the focus of this chapter will be on the spiritual level. Are we able to integrate our sufferings within our faith vision, seeing them as graces for conforming us more fully to Christ — as did Paul? I believe this is one of the greatest challenges the Gospel poses to Christians.

## Jesus and the Spirit in Redemption

We have already reflected extensively on the role of the Holy Spirit in Christian life. But what is the role of Jesus? How does it relate to the role of the Spirit? In his encyclical on the Holy Spirit John Paul II comments on the opening verses of John's Gospel: "The Word became flesh and dwelt among us." He calls attention to a truth not adequately appreciated by many Christians: the effects of the Incarnation extend to all humankind, indeed to all creation. (Italics are in original text.)

> The Incarnation of God the Son signifies the taking up into unity with God not only of human nature, but in *this human nature, in a sense, of everything that is "flesh"*: the whole humanity, the entire visible and material world. The Incarnation, then, also has a cosmic significance, a cosmic dimension. The "first-born of all creation," becoming incarnate in the individual humanity of Christ, unites in some way with the entire reality of man, which is also "flesh" — and in this reality with all "flesh," with the whole of creation.[1]

Further, the pope continues, these effects are accomplished by the Holy Spirit.

> Thus there is a supernatural "adoption," of which the source is the Holy Spirit, love and gift. *As such he is given to man.* And in the *superabundance of the uncreated gift there begins* in the heart of all human beings that particular *created gift* whereby they "become par-

takers of the divine nature." Thus human life becomes permeated, through participation, by the divine life, and itself acquires a divine, supernatural dimension.[2]

God works through the Incarnation to redeem all humankind. Our question now becomes, "What is the relationship between Jesus and the Spirit in our redemption *as Christians*?" An intimate connection exists between the work of Jesus and the work of the Spirit in our salvation. John's Gospel tell us it is Jesus that sends the Spirit, and conversely, it is the Spirit that brings us back to Jesus. Recall again Christ's words in the Last Supper Discourse, "Yet I tell you the sober truth: It is much better for you that I go. If I fail to go, the Paraclete will never come to you, whereas if I go, I will send him to you" (Jn 16:7). The Spirit is the Counselor sent by Jesus to continue the presence of Jesus on earth. John Paul II explains that the Spirit becomes another Counselor continuing the work of the first Counselor, Jesus.

> Between the Holy Spirit and Christ there thus subsists, in the economy of salvation, an intimate bond, whereby the Spirit works in human history as "another Counselor," permanently ensuring the transmission and spreading of the Good News revealed by Jesus of Nazareth. Thus, in the Holy Spirit-Paraclete, who in the mystery and action of the Church unceasingly continues the historical presence on earth of the Redeemer and his saving work, the glory of Christ shines forth, as the following words of John attest: "He [the Spirit of truth] will glorify me, for *he will take what is mine and declare it to you.*"[3]

And the *entire* effect of the redemption of Christ is now transmitted to the Spirit: "The *Redemption accomplished by the Son* in the dimensions of the earthly history of humanity . . . is . . . in its entire salvific power, transmitted to the Holy Spirit."[4] The conclusion is simple: every movement of the Holy Spirit in us is an effect of our redemption by Jesus.

Paul's letters reflect this interplay between Jesus and the Spirit. Recall that for Paul the effects of the redemption were experienced in terms of power. This power was attributed now to the Spirit, now to Jesus. For Paul the connection between the Spirit and Jesus was so intimate that he frequently interchanged the two, as he does in this well-known prayer, "May he [the Father] strengthen you inwardly through the working of his Spirit. May Christ dwell in your hearts through faith, and may charity be the root and foundation of your life" (Eph 3:16–17). For Paul it is the presence of the Spirit in the community of believers that enables it to be called the body of Christ. Having listed the various gifts given by the Spirit to individuals for the sake of the community and insisted that "it is one and the same Spirit who produces all these gifts," he concludes simply, "You, then, are the body of Christ. Every one of you is a member of it" (1 Cor 12:27). And Paul does point out that the Spirit is the source of faith in Jesus: "And no one can say 'Jesus is Lord,' except in the Holy Spirit" (1 Cor 12:3). The Spirit brings us to Jesus.

We have insisted that the only adequate view of the self is a model acknowledging God's presence, a model similar to the Scriptural Model of the self. This model situates the Spirit in the center of the self, acknowledging the Spirit's continual presence and activity. But by insisting on the centrality of the Spirit in Christian living, the Scriptural Model is simultaneously insisting on the centrality of Jesus — for the Spirit brings us to Jesus.

## Establishing a Relationship with Jesus

As Christians we enjoy a relationship with God our Father; Jesus taught us to acknowledge this relationship in the very way we pray: "Our Father who art in heaven." As Christians we enjoy also a relationship with Jesus — Jesus now raised from the dead, glorified and at the right hand of his Father in heaven. While he was alive Jesus invited his disciples to this relationship. Now through the Spirit he invites each one of us — especially in troubled times.

> Jesus said: "Come to me, all you who are weary and find life burdensome, and I will refresh you. Take my yoke upon your shoulders and learn from me, for I am gentle and humble of heart. Your souls will find rest, for my yoke is easy and my burden light" (Mt 11:28–30).

Our Christian belief in the Father and in Jesus implies not only that we assent to the dogmas concerning their existence but also that we acknowledge the relationship that this assent implies. The previous chapter highlighted the significance of the relationship for Paul. Such references dot his writings: in his letter to the Philippians he writes bluntly, "For to me, 'life' means Christ; hence dying is so much gain" (Phil 1:21).

Though most Christians can intellectually grant the existence of this relationship with Christ, we often have difficulty making it meaningful — I know I did, finding it much easier to relate and pray to God as Father. In no way, however, does a relationship with Jesus undermine our relationship with the Father: the Father and Jesus are not in competition. Indeed Jesus becomes the model for our relationship to the Father; through him, in him and with him we move to the Father. To the extent we ignore Jesus we are ignoring the purpose of the Father in sending Jesus. I believe my relationship to Jesus took a major step forward at the time of the auto accidents. My experience of Jesus as the Good Shepherd shared in Chapter II opened the door to this new dimension. As I reflect on this and other experiences I am aware of two insights fostering my new openness to Christ.

The first was a deeper appreciation of the fact discussed in Chapter IV: **Jesus is truly human.** Much of my reading about Jesus had stressed his divinity in a way that overshadowed his humanity. Unreflectively I developed an image of a Jesus that kept him outside the human condition; I did not realize that Jesus was one of us. Since I did not appreciate the truth of Jesus' humanity, I simply could not fully resonate with him. I was not able to focus on Gospel texts and allow them to bring me into a presence of Jesus — as, for instance, I did after the accidents with the Good Shepherd texts in the Gospel of John. My study of the role of the Holy Spirit in Jesus' life was a great help in removing this barrier. Books such as Marcus Borg's were great helps.[5] Eventually I realized that Jesus was indeed truly human, like us in all but sin. I returned often to the simple sentences of Vatican II: "He worked with human hands, He thought with a human mind, acted by human choice, and loved with a human heart. Born of the Virgin Mary, He has truly been made one of us, like us in all things except sin."[6]

And with a growing realization of his humanity I came to appreciate more and more a fact also reflected upon in Chapter IV: Jesus suffered. Unconsciously I had assumed that his divinity preserved him from ordinary human suffering. Though I acknowledged the suffering of the crucifixion, I had a more difficult time acknowledging Jesus' ordinary daily suffering, such as failure and loneliness. But he did suffer. Try as he might, Jesus was never successful in convincing the Jews — or his disciples — of his message. Further his own people rejected him and his specially chosen disciples abandoned him. I began to realize that his sense of exhaustion, frustration, failure and loneliness must have been acute. I began realizing that he could resonate with my experiences. When I experience exhaustion, frustration, failure, loneliness I can go to Jesus; he understands.

My second insight was equally crucial: **I relate to Jesus best when I find the image of Jesus relevant to my current situation.** It is not enough simply to acknowledge his humanness; I must find that specific aspect of his humanness that relates to my current situation — Jesus lonely when I'm lonely. This seems obvious to me now, but I believe I had an unspoken assumption that I should be able to reflect upon any passage in the Gospels and immediately be opened to the presence of Jesus. I am not certain of the origin of this assumption. It might have come from the way I was taught to pray. I was given meditation books with Gospel passages for each day of the year. I was instructed to find the current day, read the Gospel passage slowly, talk with Jesus and allow the presence of Jesus to emerge in these conversations. Usually only boredom emerged. I became discouraged about my ability to pray the Gospels and was embarrassed that I got so little from them. I felt bad that Jesus did not have a central role in my life.

When I pray to Jesus I now pray about whatever is preoccupying me. Having owned my situation I then look for the image of Jesus or the Gospel passage that speaks to it. I have developed a list of favorite passages relating to situations in my life and I return often to these same passages — such as the Good Shepherd texts. Gradually Jesus is becoming relevant to more and more aspects of my life. I should note that having established the relationship, it becomes much easier simply to sit in the presence of Jesus simply repeating his name.[7]

A recent experience illustrates these insights. I experienced the rupture of a lifelong relationship; further I experienced the rupture as a personal betrayal. (I fear many of us have similar sufferings with spouses, parents, children, friends.) I was totally unprepared for it. I continue to learn from my efforts to cope with it.

I suffered much because I treasured the relationship. I wanted to process the situation with the person, reach reconciliation and resume the relationship. The other individual didn't (or couldn't), thereby intensifying my hurt and making it more difficult to forgive. For over a year I struggled to forgive the individual, wanting to forgive as I hoped to be forgiven by God — only too aware of the petition of the Lord's Prayer: "Forgive us our trespasses *as* we forgive those who trespass against us." Though I had the desire to forgive, I found myself regularly disparaging the individual in my mind. It was clear that my "forgiveness" was not very deep. But I regularly prayed over the problem and asked God's help. My annual retreat focused on my sinfulness in not being able to forgive. I came out after the eight days of retreat more humble but still struggling to forgive more fully.

Why couldn't I forgive? I was embarrassed; as a priest I had been preaching forgiveness all my life. I had never had this problem before, because I had never experienced a similar hurt. I sought the advice of a therapist. I saw the therapist for several months and the meetings were helpful. I became aware of an unconscious pattern in my behavior toward friends. My commitment was not unconditional; it was based on reciprocity, conditioned by the behavior of others. When I deemed the behavior unacceptable, I unconsciously adjusted my commitment. I told myself — albeit unconsciously — that love must be continually earned by appropriate actions. I am now aware that the pattern is self-centered and sinful, and that I have an interior resistance — an on-going "thorn in the flesh" — that keeps me from loving unconditionally. The pattern originated in my early childhood, but it had never come to my attention before because no friend's behavior had ever reached this level of unacceptability. I did emerge from therapy with more self-knowledge; at least I understood why I was having a problem with forgiveness. But the problem remained. It was now two years since the original incident.

Sometime in the following year another event occurred. I can't even remember where or when it happened. I know it did happen because it has made all the difference even now in my being able to handle my suffering. What occurred to me was a very simple fact about Jesus: Jesus was betrayed by his friend Judas — also denied by Peter and abandoned by most disciples. That was it. Jesus knew human betrayal and abandonment! For the first time in my life I *realized* that fact. I had heard it since childhood but I had never *realized* it. So in my pain I went to Jesus betrayed and abandoned — and from the cross forgiving even those crucifying him. I resonated with Jesus. And I believe I am receiving strength through the Spirit, becoming conformed more fully to Christ in loving and forgiving at a deeper level.

I am a theology teacher and priest; I receive strength by identifying with Jesus the teacher and preacher. I identify with Jesus the teacher in his tireless efforts to convince the people of the message on the Kingdom of God; I also identify with him when his message is rejected. I know mothers and school teachers — those whose vocation is caring for children — who receive strength by identifying with Jesus in his love and respect for little children. Identification with Christ always strengthens us enabling us to serve the Kingdom of God more effectively.

Christians are disciples of Christ. The teaching in John's Gospel is addressed to the first Christian community and to us: "I am the way, and the truth, and the life; no one comes to the Father but through me" (Jn 14:6). Allowing Jesus to be our way, truth and life presumes reflection on his life. As the Gospels become our book they eventually replace the Ten Commandments as the guide for our life. Our guide is Jesus — or, as Paul put it, the law of the Spirit of Christ written on our hearts. Through the Spirit's interior guidance and strength we grow in our relationship to Christ and in our ability to follow his teaching and example. The Spirit brings us to Jesus.

### Living the Relationship in Suffering

How does Jesus save us? It is interesting to note the answer to this question has never been formally defined by the Christian Church. There have been differing understandings of how Jesus saves us through history. All indeed reflect an important aspect of Jesus' significance for us; none exhaust the full dimensions of this significance. My personal understanding has been enriched immeasurably through the growing emphasis on the role of the Holy Spirit in Christian life, an emphasis highlighted in Vatican II as well as in the pope's recent encyclical on the Holy Spirit. This book is attempting to spell out my beliefs. I've reached a rather simple conclusion: **Jesus saves us in every way that his example, teaching and presence (through the Spirit) make a difference in our lives.** Chapter II spells out the scope of the power of the Spirit sent by Jesus and the Father in Christian life; Chapter IV gives an illustration of this power in the life of Paul; the previous section gives an illustration from my own life.

The teaching, example and presence of Jesus are significant for every aspect of our lives, but it is not an exaggeration to assert that they are most necessary during times of suffering. In *good* times we can forget about our need for God's help; in *troubled* times we can't! The goal of Christian spirituality is to love and serve God and others with our entire heart and strength at *all* times. At no time in human life is this desire challenged as much as in times of suffering. At these times we tend to reverse our desire and move toward a self-pitying isolation.

The process of allowing Christ to save us from suffering has three moments. **First, we must name our sufferings.** These sufferings may be minor, our daily "thorns in the flesh," or major, our Gethsemanes and Calvarys. But naming the suffering is for many the hardest part of the process. We resist it, feeling that weakness demeans us. As the Capitalistic Model of the self illustrates, we prefer to imagine ourselves as independent and self-reliant, with no need of help from God. But the acknowledgment of our need is an essential condition for the Lord's action. Paul was painfully aware of his infirmity, his "thorn in the flesh," and his need for help. So also were the blind, the deaf, the diseased and the infirm in the Gospel. Acknowledging need is never demeaning for the disciple of Christ; rather it is a privileged occasion for experiencing his love.

**Second, we approach Christ in confidence — using images from the Gospel that are powerful for us.** Since our Christian life is now focused on the imitation of Jesus, not merely on keeping the commandments, we look to Jesus' teaching and example for guidance and to his presence for strength. And we go in confidence because Jesus invites us to come to him — *especially if we are weary and burdened.* We must get over the self-consciousness that may keep us from Jesus because we don't want to "bother" Jesus or abuse his goodness with another request. Jesus is our savior; the Father sent Jesus to help us in our need. Without his help we cannot continue to serve the Father's Kingdom: "I am the vine, you are the branches; without me you can do nothing." The Gospels indicate that the people Jesus cured, having admitted their need, approached him in total trust; lack of faith inhibited Jesus' ability to heal.

**Third, we wait patiently and confidently — days, months, even years.** Paul recalls begging the Lord three different times to remove his "thorn in the flesh." But while we are waiting we are being transformed gradually, even below the level of conscious awareness. Often there is deeper resistance to grace within us than we imagined — as I became aware in my own effort to forgive my friend. We wait confidently: "My grace is sufficient." God's grace is always stronger than our weakness — we have been redeemed!

Reflection on my own struggle to forgive presented above makes it important to add two observations on the process of being redeemed by the Lord from my suffering. First, concerning the connection between suffering and sin — though this book is concerned primarily with human suffering that is not a result of sin. Chapter I noted one dimension of suffering (the spiritual dimension) relating to sinfulness, namely, the suffering arising when we resist God's movements and are untrue to our deepest identity. But there is another connection between suffering and sin. Coping with any suffering drains our physical and psychological resources; as our energy dwindles we lose the strength to love. For example, dealing with the pain of my ruptured friendship saps my energy and I am continually tempted to lack of forgiveness. Going to Christ renews my strength at every level, physical, psychological and spiritual, enabling me to live more lovingly. I am comfortable asserting that Jesus "saves me" simultaneously from physical as well as moral weakness, from suffering as well as from sin.

John Paul II's letter "On the Christian Significance of Human Suffering" expresses well the relationship of all human weakness (physical and moral) to God's saving power. What is true for Christ, the pope assures us, is true also for the Christian.

> He [Christ] dies nailed to a cross. But if his exaltation to glory is achieved in such weakness, and this is confirmed by the power of the resurrection, this very fact demonstrates that the *weakness inherent in every human affliction* can be permeated by the power of God revealed in Christ's cross. In this context to suffer means to become particularly sensitive, and with all one's defenses down, to the operation of God's saving power which is offered in Christ to humankind. (Italics mine.)[8]

At every level of human weakness we Christians are called to become "particularly sensitive" to the power of God offered in Christ and so like him be exalted. Much as we hate to admit it, the effort to remain loving during suffering is central to our conformity to Christ and so to our maturity as Christians.

Second, our resistance to the grace of redemption is often below the level of our conscious awareness. Each of us has developed unconsciously self-centered orientations toward life beginning from our very earliest years.[9] Frequently suffering is the occasion for recognizing this resistance to grace and for opening our hearts to a deeper love of God and others. In some cases — like Ivan Ilyich's — only extreme suffering breaks down the resistance to God's grace. Thomas Keating says it well: the weakness at every level of our being can become the occasion for deeper experiences of God's mercy.

> Once we start the spiritual journey, God is totally on our side. Everything works together for our good. If we can believe this, we can save ourselves an enormous amount of trouble. Purification of the unconscious is an important part of the journey. The decision to choose the values of the gospel does not touch the unconscious motivation that is firmly in place by age three or four, and more deeply entrenched by the age of reason. As long as the false self with its emotional programs for happiness is in place, we tend to appropriate any progress in the spiritual journey to ourselves.

> The experience of God's love and the experience of our weaknesses are correlative. These are the two poles that God works with as he gradually frees us from an immature way of relating to him. The experience of our desperate need for God's healing is the measure in which we experience his infinite mercy. The deeper the experience of God's mercy, the more compassion we will have for others.[10]

Suffering exposes the need for healing often buried in our unconscious selves. My struggle to forgive my friend eventually exposed my own unconscious resistance to the Spirit. Becoming aware of this resistance is enabling Christ to save me more fully at this deep interior level.

### The Cross

Only recently have I gotten over my negative connotations to the phrase "the cross." In my experience the phrase was used to describe an attitude toward life not found in the Gospel: "Life is a vale of tears; it is supposed to be difficult because it is a trial, a testing. God sends us 'the cross' as our test. If we bear our crosses faithfully in this life we will be rewarded with eternal life in the next. Then we will be happy." I had the impression that good Christians were not supposed to be happy in this life and that the Christian attitude to this life is detachment and non-involvement because it is the next life that really counts.

Everything I have learned about the Gospels convinces me that these attitudes are not part of Jesus' message. Jesus taught us to work for the coming of the Kingdom of God with our *entire* heart, souls, minds and bodies. He even taught us to pray regularly for its coming *on earth*: "Thy Kingdom come, Thy will be done *on earth* as it is in heaven." And he showed us how to live for the Kingdom by his own life of service to others. There is no passage in the Gospels clearer about criteria for being a disciple than Matthew's Last Judgment scene: I was hungry and you gave me to eat. The conclusion: true disciples must be totally involved in life by loving and serving God and others. But Jesus did also assure his followers that a life of loving service to others in this life would be rewarded in the next.

The Gospels testify that the message Jesus preached was threatening to the established order, and so Jesus and his message are vigorously resisted. In the Gospels the cross becomes a symbol for the resistance Jesus and his disciples encountered in working for the Kingdom. Being faithful to his mission in spite of resistance brought Jesus and the disciples increasing persecution. It must have been very confusing for the disciples. He gathers them at Caesarea Phillippi before setting out on his final journey to Jerusalem. For the first time Jesus discloses his identity. He responds to Peter by acknowledging that he is, indeed, the Messiah. Quickly, however, he dispels any misunderstanding of the title; he is not a Messiah that would establish the Kingdom of God through worldly force. His reprimand of Peter couldn't be stronger.

> He began to teach them that the Son of Man had to suffer greatly and be rejected by the elders, the chief priests, and the scribes, and be killed, and rise after three days. He spoke this openly. Then Peter took him aside and began to rebuke him. At this he turned around and, looking at his disciples, rebuked Peter and said, "Get behind me, Satan. You are thinking not as God does, but as human beings do" (Mk 8:31–33).

Jesus seemed to know where his life was leading and that he would not be spared from suffering. He knew also that his disciples would not be spared.

> He summoned the crowd with his disciples and said to them, "Whoever wishes to come after me must deny himself, take up his cross and follow me. For whoever wishes to save his life will lose it, but whoever loses his life for my sake and that of the gospel will save it. What profit is there for one to gain the whole world and forfeit his life?" (Mk 8:34–36).

Without taking up the cross, no one of them could be his disciple. But the cross is not only a symbol of resistance to God's Kingdom; the cross is also a symbol of transformation. Only by denying themselves and taking up the cross would they find true life.

What is the meaning of "the cross" for Christians? What are our crosses? Our crosses are all obstacles impeding our call to imitate Christ in living fully for the Kingdom of God. Our crosses are frequently the same as our physical, psychological and spiritual sufferings. They may be internal, such as physical and moral weakness, or external, such as difficulty in relationships or resistance by others to our service. But our crosses are more than obstacles; they are obstacles carrying with them the promise of transformation — the same transformation experienced by Jesus and his disciples.

Paul deserves the last word on the value of the cross; no one in the New Testament witnesses better to its transforming power. The obstacles he experienced in being faithful to his call after Damascus come both from his internal weaknesses (the "thorn in the flesh") and from external resistance to his service. But every suffering is an occasion for experiencing the power of God — and even boasting in it. For Paul the cross is at the heart of the wisdom of God.

> The message of the cross is complete absurdity to those who are headed for ruin but to us who are experiencing salvation it is the power of God. Scripture says, "I will destroy the wisdom of the wise, and thwart the cleverness of the clever." Where is the wise man to be found? Where the scribe? Where is the master of worldly argument? Has not God turned the wisdom of this world into folly? Since in God's wisdom the world did not come to know him through "wisdom," it pleased God to save those who believe through the absurdity of the preaching of the gospel. Yes, Jews demand "signs" and Greeks look for "wisdom," but we preach Christ crucified — a stumbling block to Jews, and an absurdity to Gentiles; but to those

who are called, Jews and Greeks alike, Christ the power of God and the wisdom of God. For God's folly is wiser than men, and his weakness more powerful than men (1 Cor 1:18–25).

## REFLECTION QUESTIONS

1. How does your understanding of the redemption relate to the one presented here? What remains confusing?

2. Do you have a relationship with Jesus? Is the relationship significant? Is Jesus primarily a friend, or primarily a model, or both? Explain.

3. Can you recall the origin and development of your relationship with Jesus? What fostered this relationship — any key insights or experiences?

4. What are your major sufferings now? How can insights from this chapter help you in dealing with them?

5. Give examples of how Jesus saves you simultaneously from suffering and from sin.

6. Are you aware of having been transformed by your crosses, that is, of becoming more conformed to Christ precisely through your suffering? Give examples.

# VI. ALL-POWERFUL *AND* ALL-LOVING? A CONCLUDING REFLECTION

Frequently I am asked by students how I personally can believe in God when there is so much suffering in the world. Some students asking the question have had their faith challenged by major personal losses and have not been able to reconcile God's love with the events causing their suffering. They ask me the question in private; they are sad. Other students asking the question are looking for further reasons to reject Christianity; usually their previous experience with Christianity has been negative. They often confront me publicly in class, "You can't prove to me that God exists." They are angry. Both groups deserve answers. Their questions may be the occasion for a total rethinking and internalizing of their inherited Christian faith. Sooner or later doesn't life call every reflective believer to wrestle with the problem of God and suffering?

I am aware that this book has not responded directly to the question of reconciling Christian belief in an all-powerful and all-loving God with the presence of so much suffering and evil in the world.[1] It must be acknowledged that centuries of Christian reflection on the problem have not produced a response to the question that has gained consensus. The question remains, however, the basic intellectual barrier for many to acceptance of Christian claims about God.

This concluding chapter has two movements: the first presents the perennial problem of reconciling God and suffering and then attempts to give an intellectual response from a Christian perspective; the second suggests an approach to the power of God differing from the one traditionally used as a more helpful way of responding to the age-old problem. These remarks are likely to be the most controversial of the book. I present them not as solutions to the problem but simply as an approach that has been personally most helpful. The importance of the question demands it be treated, however inadequately. To handle this question it is necessary to interrupt the pastoral tone of the book and to engage in some sophisticated theological reasoning. Readers less interested in this intellectual argumentation can move directly to the section entitled "The Power of God."

## The Problem

The classic statement of the problem we are discussing was presented by David Hume, an eighteenth-century English philosopher, in his book *Dialogues Concerning Natural Religion.* The problem arose originally as a challenge to the Christian belief in a God who is both all-loving and all-powerful.

Is God willing to prevent evil, but not able?
Then God is impotent.
Is God able, but not willing?
Then God is malevolent.
Is God both able and willing?
Whence, then is evil?

An expanded restatement of the problem by Nelson Pike in the first paragraph of his book *God and Evil* is helpful.

> If God is omnipotent, then He could prevent evil if He wanted to. And if God is perfectly good, then He would want to prevent evil if He could. Thus, if God exists and is both omnipotent and perfectly good, then there exists a being who could prevent evil if he wanted to, and who would want to prevent evil if he could. And if this last is true, how can there be so many evils in the world? This, in broad outline, is the traditional theological problem of evil.[2]

The problem as it arose initially in the modern age was posed by eighteenth-century intellectuals who had explicitly rejected the validity of the Christian faith and viewed reason alone as an adequate approach to reality. Indeed, the question as posed was hostile to faith and intended to undermine its claims by dwelling upon a seeming incompatibility. It is important to remember that when we ask the question today we are asking it in a totally different context. *As believing Christians,* we are attempting to reconcile God's love and human suffering. The real question for us becomes: How can human reasoning *complement* our religious convictions and experiences? Emphatically, the agnostic formulation of the question is not our own. I agree with Douglas John Hall's observations.

> Such a formulation of the question . . . obscures its most existential dimension, which is the identity and the condition of the one who asks it. The poem of Job is a paradigmatic and unforgettable grappling with the problem of God and human suffering because it is not theoretical, but a drama in which the identity of all those who put the question, especially Job himself, is revealed in detail. . . . No human question is ever asked (and no answer given) in a historical vacuum; it is asked in a specific time and place by specific persons. With certain kinds of questions this contextual dimension may not be so significant; but with our present question it is of primary importance. The aspects of the problem of suffering which we shall hold up, as well as the responses that we shall give to them, will be determined in great measure by the particular circumstances, openly acknowledged or silently assumed, in which we find ourselves.[3]

The existential situation influencing my reflections has been spelled out in the preceding chapters.

## A Christian Response

I begin my attempt to respond to students' questions on God's relationship to suffering by candidly admitting that my faith does not rest upon finding a satisfying intellectual response to their question. I even acknowledge that I am not able to supply one using reason alone. I begin by sharing with students why I am a Christian in the first place. My response is primarily a witness to God's presence in my life; it is not an argument. Only if I perceive that they find me credible as a person and so are willing to accept my witness as an legitimate interpretation of human experience do I proceed to deal with the question of God's relationship to suffering. No one ever wins an argument on religion; in earlier years I spent much energy "losing" such arguments with students. The following is my response, *a* Christian response, not *the* Christian response.

Commitment to any ultimate meaning system is based on the fact that it enhances life. Why am I a Christian? Why do I remain a Christian? The simple answer is: I experience God with me in good times and in bad. As a young person I was taught intellectually about Christianity; as a young adult I progressively understood, experienced and committed myself to the Christian world view. I became aware that the heart of faith was not merely an acceptance of a set of doctrines but a personal commitment to the reality they proclaimed — the Father, Jesus, the Spirit, the community of believers. I am aware of experiencing the presence of God and Jesus — both personally and within the Christian community — in a way that has made a significant difference in my life. As I grew I became more able to articulate the difference my faith made for my life. I am now comfortable asserting that to the extent I am faithful to living the Gospel I experience enrichment of my life; to the extent I am not faithful I experience diminishment. In short, I am not a Christian on the basis of rational argument but on the basis of experiences I interpret in light of the Gospel — an interpretation which is itself a gift of the Holy Spirit. These experiences of God are present also, perhaps even especially, in times of suffering.

Only within this context can I attempt to give a response to the question about how I personally reconcile my belief in an all-powerful and all-loving God with so much suffering in the world. I acknowledge that the argument presented is of little help in the midst of great suffering. It may, however, be helpful afterward in processing the suffering as well as in helping remove barriers to God in dealing with subsequent suffering. Its value is primarily for those of us who accept Christian beliefs and want to show others — and ourselves — that there is a way to complement our faith convictions using human reasoning.

My intention is to present in outline form — a complete discussion would entail another book — an approach that is common to several Christian theologians, though like myself each gives it a distinctive "slant." The basic inspiration is from John Hick's *Evil and the God of Love;* Brian Hebblethwaite's *Evil, Suffering, and Religion* has been helpful for grasping Hick.[4] Hick's approach is highly sophisticated; it is beyond the purpose of the book to present Hick's full argumentation — not to mention the standard critiques of his position.[5] At the outset I acknowledge I am not fully comfortable with any approach to our problem. I do find myself, however, "less uncomfortable" with Hick — given crucial modifications — than with others. The presentation of the argument is my own; I have organized it around three questions: 1) **What is God's purpose in creating us?** 2) **What does God** *directly will* **to achieve this purpose?** 3) **What does God** *merely permit*? I depart from Hick in responding to the last question.

1) **What is God's purpose in creating us?** Please recall we are reflecting as believing Christians and therefore presuming God's revelation contained in Scripture. An adequate response to this question is essential before approaching the two following questions. Rather surprisingly I have found that many of us — including myself — entertain assumptions not found in Scripture. Unreflectively we assume that God's purpose is to provide an environment conducive to the greatest happiness and least pain. But this is not the response given in either the Old or New Testaments. Summarizing the Law and the Prophets Jesus presents God's purpose in terms of the two great commandments, love of God and of our neighbor. Jesus also presents it in terms of God's will and God's Kingdom; but the Gospels teach us that God's will and Kingdom are present on earth to the extent that we love God and our neighbor. God's purpose in creating the world is to provide an environment in which we humans can fulfill the purpose of our existence by freely choosing to love and serve God and others — and in this way be rewarded with eternal life in heaven. Significantly God's purpose is not presented in Scripture as providing an environment conducive to the greatest happiness and least pain. Indeed the Gospels seems to presume that following Jesus faithfully would entail much suffering. Note the Beatitudes.

2) **What does God** *directly will* **in order to achieve this purpose?** In other words, what conditions are necessary to fulfill the purpose of creation? If the conditions are necessary for fulfilling God's purpose, so the theological reasoning goes, God must will them directly. The response to the question: to fulfill the purpose of our existence God directly wills that we humans be endowed with the following two characteristics: *freedom* and *materiality*.

Why *freedom*? The Bible does seem clear on this. The story of Adam and Eve is symbolic of the human condition. Human beings are not puppets of God. Humans are given a choice whether or not to serve God. From the beginning God created us to serve God by keeping God's commandments; from the beginning we humans freely chose to disobey God by breaking God's commandments. The Bible is full of stories of obedience and disobedience to God's call; God forces no one to respond. Reflection upon our own experience confirms the fact of personal freedom: each of us is confronted daily with options for living the Gospel; we are aware of making some of these choices well and others poorly.

Why *materiality*? The question is: Why does God will a material created world at all as opposed to a world comprised of spirits not dependent upon matter, such as the angelic world? Hick reasons that since God directly wills human freedom God must also will human materiality. Why? Materiality is an essential condition for human freedom. If we knew God directly, face-to-face as it were, we would be so attracted to God we would be incapable of choosing not to love and serve God. We would lose our freedom. Consequently God must put a "veil" between God and ourselves to protect our freedom. The veil is our materiality. Hebblethwaite is commenting on Hick's argument.

> In order to have a certain relative independence of being and knowledge from their creator, created persons must have, as it were, a footing in reality at a distance from the creator, and if they are to be genuinely free and individual selves, their knowledge of God must be indirectly, even arduously, acquired, rather than thrust upon them from the beginning. The personal being of creatures, in other words, necessarily requires some such kind of context as is provided by a material evolving universe, which builds up from the simplest energies an ordered environment for personal life and growth. Personal beings, so constructed, have the chance, in such an environment, to be themselves before being wooed or called into relation with their maker. The physical world is indeed a veil between God and his creatures.[6]

As a note it should be added that the material universe, though governed by physical laws, is flexible enough to be open to evolution. We live in a physical universe that is regularly structured yet continually evolving. Indeed, we human beings see ourselves as relatively recent newcomers within this evolutionary process.

God wills a material created world to ensure human freedom. But God wills materiality for other reasons as well. First, God wills materiality as a means of revealing God's self to human beings and so leading us back to God. This reason is alluded to throughout the Old and New

Testaments; Job 38–41 quoted in Chapter III is a perfect example. Also many of the psalms:

> O Lord, our Lord, how awesome is your name through all the earth!
> You have set your majesty above the heavens!
> When I see your heavens, the work of your fingers,
>     the moon and the stars that you set in place —
> What are humans that you are mindful of them,
>     mere mortals that you care for them? (Ps 8:2, 4–5).

Paul reminds us that the creation points to its Creator. Paul asserts that all people have evidence of God's reality, "For what can be known about God is evident to them, because God made it evident to them. Ever since the creation of the world, his invisible attributes of eternal power and divinity have been able to be understood and perceived in what he has made" (Rom 1:19–20).

And second — and assuredly the most controversial aspect of Hick's approach — God wills materiality in order to provide a challenging context for the formation of human character. The challenges to human growth arise both from human freedom and from human materiality. Human growth is fostered both by the struggle to choose good over evil and by the effort to persevere in doing good despite obstacles. The challenge to growth posed by freedom is obvious; daily we wrestle with moral choices. Less obvious is the challenge posed by materiality. Materiality refers to all the obstacles to growth related to our material condition — most especially to physical pain. Hard as it is for us to accept, there seems to be a dimension of physical pain connected with the human condition that God directly wills. It is inherent in the human life cycle — being born, growing and maturing, aging and dying. It is also the result of all the forces affecting us in our material dimension: hunger and thirst, fear and anxiety, disease and accident, fire and flood.

Hick draws support for his argument from the second-century Christian writer St. Irenaeus who emphasized that God intended to create the world as an environment challenging to human survival and so more conducive to "soul-making." Irenaeus understood that these challenges for building character would be both moral and physical and that human growth would be achieved only through painful trial and error. He believed that by handling these challenges well, God intended us to grow from the "image of God" by our creation into an ever fuller "likeness of God." S. Paul Schilling, a theologian influenced by Hick, addresses the role of physical pain in God's intention.

> Physical pain and other forms of suffering not clearly caused by sin are also best understood if the world that contains them is seen as a vale of soul-making. If our environment were radically altered into a soft, easy, unchallenging order, it would produce "a soft, unchallenged race of men." A painless world would exclude physical and mental toil, hunger and thirst, and extremes of heat and cold. But it would also render needless the activities by which people meet these painful exigencies — hunting, agriculture, construction of shelter, and social organization. It would likewise exclude the painful effort needed for the advancement of knowledge and pursuit of the arts, drastically altering the nature of human life and thus eliminating the creative enterprises that make life most valuable. Presumably God might have made a world without pain, but in so doing he would have destroyed the possibility of creating souls capable of realizing high values in fellowship with him and with each other.[7]

Hall, though never referring to Hick, reaches similar conclusions. He identifies four types of suffering inherent in the human condition and so directly intended by God as a context to foster human growth. Reflecting upon the story of Adam and Eve and the temptation by the serpent in the garden Hall isolates four conditions of human existence leading inevitably to human suffering: the experiences of loneliness, limitation, temptation and anxiety.

> What I am contending is that there are, in fact, forms of suffering which belong, in God's intention, to the human condition. Not *all* of what we experience as suffering is totally absurd, a mistake, an oversight, or the consequence of sin. There is something about a significant portion of the suffering through which we pass that belongs to the very foundations of being — something without which our human being would not and could not be what it is meant to be.[8]

Having explained the values inherent in the four types of suffering, Hall concludes that suffering is necessary for human growth.

What we are admitting, surely, in such reflections as these, is that life without any kind of suffering would be no life at all; it would be a form of death. Life — the life of the spirit like the life of the body — depends in some mysterious way upon *the struggle to be*. This presupposes, as the condition necessary to life itself, the presence of life's antithesis, that is, of that which threatens or negates, circumscribes or challenges. This is where evolutionary theory and creational theology *do* converge, and in a provocative and unusual manner. Both evolution and creation presuppose that there is a struggle involved in existence, and that this struggle is basically positive, even though it contains strongly negative dimensions.[9]

Theologians agree that a primary "soul-making" value of suffering is enhanced empathy with the suffering of others. Suffering has a unique capacity to break the bonds of our individualism and to insert us more deeply into the human community as co-sufferers. To the degree we acknowledge our own pain can we become empathetic with the pain of others.

**3) What does God *merely permit* in order to achieve the purpose of creation?** In responding to this question I am departing somewhat from Hick. He does not put similar emphasis on the distinction between "directly willing" and "merely permitting." Since I can accept the fact that human freedom and materiality are necessary to fulfill God's purpose for us, I am forced to acknowledge that each is open to a side-effect that God may not directly will but must permit to achieve the purpose: from freedom, *moral evil* (sin) and from materiality, *excessive pain and suffering*.

At this point in the argument difficulties begin multiplying, difficulties I find impossible to respond to from human reason alone. For instance, the distinction between "directly willing" and "merely permitting" is troublesome. Wouldn't God be fully aware of the consequences of freedom and materiality and so in some sense directly will them? Equally troublesome is the distinction between "*acceptable* pain," that is, pain inherent in the human condition and conducive to "soul-making," and "*excessive* pain," pain which seems beyond the intention of the Creator because it is not conducive to "soul-making."[10] Wouldn't God be aware that the results of human freedom and materiality would be *excessive* suffering for much of humanity and so in some way want to alter that result?

Why *moral evil*? Sin is a by-product of the gift of freedom. Sin proceeds entirely from human choice; the Holy Spirit (God) moves us only toward good. Clearly God cannot will moral evil and therefore must merely permit it in order to achieve the purpose of creation. And from our very beginning God has permitted us to abuse our freedom and to sin: Adam and Eve, Cain and Abel, the Tower of Babel, Noah and the Flood. Reflection upon the human condition today reveals how monstrously — as individuals and as societies — we continue to abuse this freedom. Yet as we've seen the very struggle to choose good over evil is itself intended by God because it provides the environment conducive to "soul-making"; and so in some sense good comes from the struggle. In short, God *directly wills* the human condition but *merely permits* its abuse. Troublesome for many is the total freedom of choice God allows humans. Shouldn't God put an upper limit on our ability to abuse freedom?

Why *excessive pain and suffering*? Recall that by excessive we mean suffering (physical, psychological, spiritual) inherent in the human condition but not conducive to "soul-making." The suffering of children is a heart-rending example. No one familiar with the Christian belief about God's love — not to mention experiencing this love personally — can say that God directly wills the monstrous sufferings we observe in our world. Yet honesty forces us to acknowledge the existence of such excessive sufferings; the daily news is a painful awakener. Yesterday's news was almost entirely dominated by reports of war and starvation in two nations and by the devastating effects of an earthquake and a flood in two others. Since such sufferings exist, God, as the creator and sustainer of the created universe, must permit them. I share the views of two previously quoted theologians, Schilling and Hall.

On the positive side, it is clear that evil and suffering often contribute significantly to the growth of persons as realizers of value. However, the problems encountered, particularly the reality of excessive pain and the role of suffering in frustrating, undermining, and debasing persons, make it unsound to hold that an all-powerful, all-wise, and perfectly good God purposes or permits evil *in order to* produce worthy persons. Such a God would presumably have open to him means of achieving his creative ends that would not require so vast a burden of anguish.[11]

It may be the intention of the Creator, according to biblical religion, that the human creature should experience dimensions of deprivation, struggle, and insecurity in order to make good the deeper promise of its creaturehood; but by no stretch of the imagination could anyone accuse the tradition of positing a God who actually wills the massive, unbearable, or seemingly absurd suffering of the creature — *any* creature! A deity personally and directly responsible for all the agony of earth would be unrecognizable as God from the perspective of biblical faith.[12]

Where do we draw the line between *acceptable* and *excessive* suffering? Shouldn't God put a limit on the amount of suffering we are expected to endure? Shouldn't God at least spare children? Again theological reasoning fails to provide a satisfactory response.

How can we reconcile our belief in an all-powerful and all-loving God with the presence of so much evil and suffering in the world? I find Hick's insights on our first two questions very helpful. They replaced my previous assumptions — assumptions never explicitly reflected upon — that a loving God could not directly intend *any* kind of suffering. Perhaps a rampant American materialistic mentality had lulled me into believing that the purpose of life is to grow in the ability to experience "the good life" (the "pursuit of happiness" through ever increasing health and wealth and fame and fortune) and that any obstacle to this must be beyond God's intentions. I am growing to appreciate more and more that the difficulties encountered in the struggle to live a Christian life are not absurd but are indeed part of God's intention for our progressive transformation into Christ. On my better days I can accept personal sufferings — the tragic automobile deaths of our students, the ruptured friendships, the daily frustrations involved in teaching, committee meetings, writing — as not absurd but indeed central to my personal "soul-making," that is, to my conformity to Christ and to my empathy with my suffering sisters and brothers.

However, in responding to the third question I have departed from Hick's argumentation. Hick views excessive suffering as an incidental by-product of the material and evolutionary created order but does not elaborate upon the distinction between what God wills and what God permits. He is able to maintain a belief in God's goodness in spite of individual suffering only by questioning the traditional Christian doctrine of eternal punishment and by insisting that in the end God rewards every person with eternal happiness.

I believe that *all* intellectual attempts to reconcile God and suffering flounder when dealing with *excessive* suffering. Distinguishing between what God directly wills and merely permits is an attempt, albeit inadequate, to cope with this problem. No rational argument has provided a satisfactory response to this problem; I doubt that it ever will. Human reason can only go so far; it can complement faith but never replace it. We are left with the same conundrum experienced by Paul.

> Oh, the depth of the riches and wisdom and knowledge of God! How inscrutable are his judgments and how unsearchable his ways! "For who has known the mind of the Lord or who has been his counselor?" (Rom 11:33–34).

## The Power of God

For myself the decisive response to the question of reconciling God and suffering is not given by the theological considerations just presented but by a reconsideration of the entire problem with a different understanding of the power of God. Recall that the assumptions of our discussion have been taken from eighteenth-century secular philosophers, philosophers with biases against Christianity.[13] Among these assumptions is a particular understanding of God and of God's power. Schilling is helpful.

> According to this view, the deity is external to and detached from the world; he creates it and sets it in motion but governs its operations from the outside. Likewise, the God rejected by many atheists has been conceived as a being above or beyond the region of natural and human existence, yet ruling it by his arbitrary will.[14]

Many discussions of the problem accept uncritically this understanding of God's relationship to the world.

The fully Christian approach to understanding suffering, however, does not; it affirms God's continual activity within the cosmos. Again Schilling:

> The Creator is not a sculptor fashioning a statue or a cobbler making
> a shoe; he is rather the Spirit who informs and interpenetrates his
> creation from within, so that it depends at every moment on his en-
> ergizing activity. He is the ground of all being and becoming, the
> matrix of all cosmic reality.[15]

An adequate understanding of God's relationship to this world demands
acknowledgment of God's power in continually energizing the entire
cosmos, human and non-human. John Paul II's encyclical on the Holy
Spirit emphasizes this truth with its insistence on the role of the Spirit
in creation itself: "This biblical concept of creation includes not only
the call to existence of the very being of the cosmos, that is to say *the
giving of existence,* but also the presence of the Spirit of God in creation,
that is to say the beginning of God's salvific self-communication to the
things he creates."[16] Any thoroughly Christian approach must acknowledge
God not only as creating the universe but also as continually sustaining
it in existence and acting within it.

And this leads us back to the opening question of Chapter II:
"How do we *expect* God to act in our world and to work in our daily
lives?" Do we focus on God's power working outside human beings in
the created universe or on God's power working within human beings
through the Holy Spirit? While continually acknowledging God as the
creator and sustainer of the universe, I *expect* God to act in my life
primarily through the power of the Spirit. In so doing I simultaneously
choose to approach our present topic within the support context mindset. The support context approach insists that God acts through the Spirit
transforming human hearts and conforming them more fully into the
likeness of Christ. I justify this approach by its prevalence in the New
Testament. Paul's prayer for his readers in Ephesians catches the heart
of my understanding.

> For this reason I kneel before the Father, from whom every family in
> heaven and on earth is named, that he may grant you in accord with
> the riches of his glory to be *strengthened with power through his Spirit
> in the inner self.* . . . (Eph 3:14–16; italics added).

I am convinced that only by understanding the power of God as a power
strengthening the inner self are we able to respond to the traditional problem of reconciling God and suffering. God remains both all-powerful

and all-loving even in suffering because the strength of God's Spirit is sufficient for every need! Perhaps this alternative understanding of the power of God begs the question as traditionally posed, but at least the begging of the question has the merit of being in continuity with an understanding of the power of God as found in the New Testament.

And this approach can only be founded upon a model of the self that acknowledges this presence and power of the Spirit within the self — a model similar to the Scriptural Model of the self used throughout this book. The power of the Spirit to strengthen the inner self has been central to every chapter of this book. Chapter II examined two models of the self for the Spirit's presence and absence, the Scriptural Model and the Capitalistic Model, and concluded that the New Testament supports the Scriptural Model, the self-in-God model. Chapter III on the Old Testament reviewed all God's reasons for causing suffering and concluded that none of them applied to Job; God's only response to Job was a heightened personal experience of God's presence. Chapter IV examined the Spirit's centrality in the lives of Jesus and of Paul, especially in their dealing with suffering. And Chapter V highlighted the importance of a personal relationship with Jesus in fully experiencing the redemption from suffering through the power of the Spirit sent by Jesus and the Father.

For me any approach to reconciling God and suffering using the meaning context mindset is less helpful. Whether I seek God's reasons for causing or permitting suffering from Scripture directly or through a reasoned argumentation compatible with Scripture, I arrive at the same impasse: arguments about God's relationship to suffering based on the power of God to control history and creation are unsatisfactory, always contradictory to my personal experience of God's love. Further many of these arguments flow from models of the self (similar to the Capitalistic Model of the self) that fail to recognize God's working within the self.

Hall and Schilling seem to support the approach I am suggesting, though neither puts a similar emphasis on the role of the Spirit. Hall acknowledges the inadequacy of all merely intellectual solutions to the problem. The response to the problem of God's relationship to suffering is not an argument but a Presence.

> Of answers to the "problem of suffering" there is in fact no lack! Only, all of them flounder on the rocks of reality, at the cry of one starving

or derelict child. The only satisfying answer is the answer given to Job — the answer that is not answer but is the presence of an Answerer. It does not matter that the Answerer brings more questions than answers; for the answer is not the words as such but the living Word — the Presence itself. The answer is the permission that is given in the Presence to be what one is, to express the dereliction that belongs to one's age and place, to share all of it with this Other: to *trample!* Faith is the communion of the spirit with this fellow sufferer, this One whose otherness lies in the fact that he will not turn away in the face of one's failure, or the failure of one's world.[17]

Nothing is assured about the outcome — or, rather, one thing only is assured, and that is that the Creator will be with the creature as it moves into the future. From the creature's side, therefore, one thing above all is called for: *trust*. Trust that God will not desert it, that its requirements will be met as they are felt — in short, the kind of trust that Jesus was getting at in his famous sermon, "Do not be anxious . . . consider the lilies . . . the birds of the air. . . . Sufficient unto the day. . . ."[18]

Schilling calls for a reconsideration of our understanding of the nature of God.[19] Our understanding of God has been dominated by Greek philosophy; in it God and Christ are situated above the world in an eternal sphere unaffected by human trials, unchangeable and immovable. But the Scriptures reveal that God is personally involved with creation. Schilling believes that God is not only present to us in our suffering but that God also suffers with us.

When human beings suffer from their own misuse of freedom, he suffers with them, not because he takes part in their evil choices, but because he is grieved by their rejection and loss of the good he wills. When they are exposed to pain through the carelessness or oppressive cruelty of others in an interdependent universe, he feels their misery deeply. When they endure hardships because of the regular functioning of a dependable natural order, he is present in their distress. And when the full exercise of his power does not prevent injury to creatures he loves, he suffers with them. The world's travail is his also.[20]

We are therefore led irresistibly to the conviction that God's loving relation to his creation includes sharing its pain. This does not mean

that we naively imagine God to suffer precisely as we do. Since he
has no nervous system, his endurance of pain cannot be simply equat-
ed with our own. . . . If human experience offers a clue to the ground
of our existence, there must be a dimension there akin to what we
know as feeling, including feelings of anguish. Something like a cross
is an ultimate reality in the universe. Ours is not an easy world, but
one that entails struggle, pathos, and suffering for both God and his
creatures.[21]

Schilling illustrates his view by citing a passage from *Night* by Elie
Wiesel, an Auschwitz survivor. The Nazi SS are hanging three Jews, two
men and a boy.

Standing behind Wiesel, another prisoner asked, "Where is God:
Where is He?" Though the adults died quickly, the child, being lighter
in weight, dangled for a half hour, struggling between life and death.
The agonizing question was repeated: "Where is God now?" Wiesel
heard a voice behind him answer: "Where is He? Here He is — He
is hanging here on this gallows."[22]

## My Grace Is Sufficient for You

Only in recent years have I had the courage to accept my suffering
as part of God's intention for my growth. My previous assumption was
that God could not possibly want *any* suffering for *any*body — and so
I prayed to have my sufferings taken away. But God doesn't take away
suffering — not for Paul, not for Jesus. God transforms us through it.
I now pray to embrace my sufferings as privileged occasions for experiencing God's power and becoming more fully conformed to Christ.

I keep returning to Paul's "thorn in the flesh," reflecting on Paul's
witness to the Corinthians when his right to minister had been challenged. After a string of boasts validating his credentials to minister
flowing from God's favors to him — including the appearance on the
way to Damascus as well as other mystical experiences — Paul concludes with his final boast.

Therefore that I might not become too elated, a thorn in the flesh
was given to me, an angel of Satan, to beat me, to keep me from being
too elated. Three times I begged the Lord about this, that it might

leave me, but he said, *"My grace is sufficient for you,* for power is made perfect in weakness." I will rather boast most gladly of my weaknesses, in order that the power of Christ may dwell with me. Therefore, I am content with weaknesses, insults, hardships, persecutions, and constraints, for the sake of Christ; for when I am weak, then I am strong (2 Cor 12:7–11; italics mine).

I also reconsider his witness to the community in Rome, a community experiencing persecution and death for its faith. Paul's experience convinces him that the power of God is stronger than any human — or non-human — force.

If God is for us, who can be against us? He who did not spare his own Son but handed him over for us all, how will he not also give us everything else along with him?. . . What will separate us from the love of Christ? Will anguish, or distress, or persecution, or famine, or nakedness, or peril, or the sword? As it is written: "For your sake we are being slain all the day; we are looked upon as sheep to be slaughtered." No, in all these things we conquer overwhelmingly through him who loved us. For I am convinced that neither death, nor life, nor angels, nor principalities, nor present things, nor future things, nor powers, nor height, or depth nor any other creature will be able to separate us from the love of God in Christ Jesus our Lord (Rom 8:31–32, 35–39).

Where is our God in suffering? We Christians do not have a fully satisfying explanation for why the world contains so much suffering. But we have something better: we have the power to deal with the suffering. We *know* where our God is during suffering. Our God is with us: with the Jewish boy on the gallows, with Ivan Ilyich in sickness, with Job in adversity, with Paul in weakness and persecution, with Jesus in crucifixion — with us in all the senseless accidents and ruptured relationships and interior brokenness of our lives. And we cannot claim to be living a fully Christian life until we believe and live this dimension of the Gospel, until we trust God's presence and power working through our own "thorns in the flesh," Gethsemanes and Calvarys.

The Jesuit poet Gerard Manley Hopkins reminds us of a simple truth of *all* being in his poem "Kingfishers."[23]

> Each mortal being does one thing and the same:
> Deals out that being indoors each one dwells;
> Selves — goes itself; *myself* it speaks and spells;
> Crying *What I do is me: for this I came.*

And he reminds us of the simple truth of all *human* being.

> I say more: the just man justices;
> Keeps grace: that keeps all his goings graces;
> Acts in God's eye what in God's eye he is —
> Christ — for Christ plays in ten thousand places,
> Lovely in limbs, and lovely in eyes not his
> To the Father through the features of men's faces.

Our God is with us through the Holy Spirit. To the degree we respond to God's Spirit we live in God, fulfill the promise of our creation and become conformed to Christ — in good times and in troubled times.

## REFLECTION QUESTIONS

1. How do you reconcile the existence of an all-loving and all-powerful God with the presence of so much evil and suffering in the world? Do you agree or disagree with the argument presented? Discuss.

2. Do you experience God's being with you in your suffering? Do you believe with Schilling that God actually suffers with you? Discuss.

3. Do you believe that God's grace is always sufficient for handling suffering well? Discuss.

4. Has suffering been a positive value in your life, that is, has it contributed to your conformity with Christ? Give examples. Explain.

# NOTES

## I. Where Is God in Suffering?

1. Thomas F. O'Dea, *The Sociology of Religion* (Englewood Cliffs: Prentice-Hall, 1966). I have used this text as background on the functional approach to understanding societal institutions.

2. I have listed Abraham Maslow's hierarchy of needs. The hierarchy is explained in his book *Motivation and Personality* (New York: Harper & Row, 1970).

3. Leo Tolstoy, "The Death of Ivan Ilyich" (New York: Bantam Books, 1981).

4. Tolstoy, pp. 126–127.

5. Tolstoy, pp. 132–133.

6. Viktor E. Frankl, *Man's Search for Meaning* (New York: Washington Square Press, 1970), pp. 121–122.

7. Elisabeth Kübler-Ross' *On Death and Dying* (New York: Macmillan, 1969). The book's primary concern is with the psychological dimension of dealing with suffering; I have extended her insights to religion.

8. I have found Tolstoy's "The Death of Ivan Ilyich" an excellent way to illustrate the process of coping with suffering from Denial through Acceptance.

9. Tolstoy, p. 118.

10. Kübler-Ross, p. 113.

11. This book is addressed primarily to Christians. To highlight the difference between the Old and New Testaments it seems helpful to use the designation *Old Testament* rather than the more scholarly acceptable *Hebrew Scriptures.*

12. Harold S. Kushner, *When Bad Things Happen to Good People* (New York: Avon, 1981).

13. *In His Spirit: A Guide to Today's Spirituality* (Mahwah: Paulist Press, 1982); *Moving in the Spirit: Becoming a Contemplative in Action* (Mahwah: Paulist Press, 1986). These books expand key insights into the Holy Spirit and further develop some of insights contained in Chapter II.

14. Daniel J. Simundson, *Faith under Fire: How the Bible Speaks to Us in Times of Suffering* (San Francisco: HarperSanFrancisco, 1991), p. 80.

## II. How Does God Work in the World?

1. My thinking has been stimulated by the following book: Brian Hebblethwaite, *Evil, Suffering and Religion* (New York: Hawthorne Books, 1976). Ch. 6, "Divine Providence," presents a version of my categories.

2. In my two previous books I have called this model the *Western Model.* The Western Model is identical with the Capitalistic Model. The latter designation simply calls attention to one aspect of the models — the *material rewards* of wealth and health earned by good deeds and expected from God for religious fidelity.

3. John Paul II, *Lord and Giver of Life,* May 30, 1986 (United States Catholic Conference: Washington, DC), para. 11.

4. *Lord and Giver of Life,* para. 12.

5. All Scripture quotes are from the *New American Bible* (Nashville: Thomas Nelson, 1986) unless otherwise noted.

6. I have dealt with these models more fully in my two previous books: *In His Spirit: A Guide to Today's Spirituality* (Mahwah: Paulist Press, 1982) and *Moving in the Spirit: Becoming a Contemplative in Action* (Mahwah: Paulist Press, 1986). Especially helpful are the first two chapters of each of the books.

7. Ira Progoff, *At a Journal Workshop* (New York; Progoff, 1980).

8. Max Weber's *The Protestant Ethic and the Spirit of Capitalism* (New York: Charles Scribner, 1958) is the classic expression of this "Puritan ethic."

9. Walter Abbott, ed., *The Documents of Vatican II* (New York: Guild, 1966), "Pastoral Constitution on the Church in the Modern World," n. 22.

10. Ch. 2, "Recognizing the Holy Spirit," and Ch. 3, "Obstacles to the Spirit," of my book *Moving in the Spirit* deal with this criterion in detail.

11. Quotes from *The New American Bible,* Confraternity of Christian Doctrine edition, 1970.

### III. Why Me, O God? Old Testament Insights

1. Carlo Carretto, *Why, O Lord? The Inner Meaning of Suffering* (Maryknoll: Orbis, 1985).

2. Carretto, p. 4.

3. Carretto, p. 78.

4. Carretto, p. 78.

5. Carretto, p. 79.

6. Carretto, p. 84.

7. My thinking has been helped by the chapter on Judaism found in the following textbook, John Bowker, *Problems of Suffering in Religions of the World* (Cambridge: Cambridge University Press, 1970).

8. Klaus Koch, "Is There a Doctrine of Retribution in the Old Testament?" from *Theodicy in the Old Testament,* James L. Crenshaw, ed. (Philadelphia: Fortress, 1983), p. 74.

9. H. H. Schmid, "Creation, Righteousness, and Salvation: Creation Theology as the Broad Horizon of Biblical Theology," from *Creation in the Old Testament,* B. Anderson, ed. (Philadelphia: Fortress Press, 1986), p. 106.

10. Roland Murphy, *The Tree of Life* (New York: Doubleday, 1990), p. 117.

11. Harold S. Kushner, *When Bad Things Happen to Good People* (New York: Avon, 1981), p. 3.

12. In the judgment of Scripture scholars, the Book of Daniel contains the only credible references to an afterlife in the entire Hebrew Bible.

13. Other Old Testament works also challenge the covenant perspective: Ecclesiastes, Jeremiah, Lamentations of Jeremiah.

14. James L. Crenshaw, *Old Testament Wisdom: An Introduction* (Atlanta: John Knox Press, 1981), pp. 124–125.

15. H. H. Rowley, "The Intellectual Versus the Spiritual Solution," taken from *The Dimensions of Job,* Nahum N. Glatzer, ed. (New York: Schocken Books, 1969), p. 125.

16. Rowley, pp. 125–126.

17. Rowley, pp. 127–128.

18. Daniel J. Simundson, *Where Is God in My Suffering?* (Minneapolis: Augsburg Publishing House, 1983), p. 42.

19. Kushner, pp. 29–30.

20. In the discipline of Formal Logic this is called a fallacy, the *post hoc ergo propter hoc* fallacy.

## IV. Strength in Suffering: New Testament Insights

1. Marcus J. Borg, *Jesus, a New Vision* (San Francisco: Harper & Row, 1988), p. 27. Borg's book is a superb presentation on Jesus' role in his culture as well as on the role of the Spirit in Jesus.

2. Borg, p. 150.

3. Borg, p. 48.

4. Borg, p. 32.

5. Roger Haight, "The Case for Spirit Christology," *Theological Studies,* Vol. 53 (1992), pp. 257–287. This article contains a fine summary of Spirit Christology as well as many footnotes to recent treatments of Jesus' relationship to the Spirit. For a response and critique to Haight see John H. Wright, "Note: Roger Haight's Spirit Christology," *Theological Studies,* Vol. 53 (1992), pp. 729–735.

6. Leon-Joseph Cardinal Suenens taken from John C. Haughey, *The Conspiracy of God: The Holy Spirit in Men* (New York: Doubleday, 1973), Preface, p. x.

7. Borg, pp. 50–51.

8. Borg, Preface.

9. "Pastoral Constitution on the Church in the Modern World," para. 22, taken from *The Documents of Vatican II* (New York: Guild Press, 1966), Walter M. Abbott, ed., pp. 220–221.

10. Borg, p. 82.

11. Borg, p. 136.

12. Raymond E. Brown, *A Crucified Christ in Holy Week: Essays on the Four Gospel Passion Narratives* (Collegeville: Liturgical Press, 1986), pp. 43–44.

13. Thomas H. Tobin, S.J., *The Spirituality of Paul* (Wilmington: Michael Glazier, 1985), p. 64. This excellent book examines Paul's

spirituality in reference to the power of God in Paul's thought: law, ethics, community, death, suffering.

14. See 1 Cor 11:16–29; 1 Cor 6:3–10; 2 Cor 11:23–29.

15. Tobin, "The Meaning and Present Value of Suffering," pp. 153–160.

16. Victor Paul Furnish, *II Corinthians: A New Translation with Introduction and Commentary,* The Anchor Bible (New York: Doubleday, 1984), pp. 548–550. This commentary identifies the thorn as a chronic though not debilitating physical malady. Furnish gives an excellent commentary on the passages we are discussing, pp. 484–552.

17. Furnish, pp. 550–551.

## V. Suffering with Christ: How Jesus Saves Us

1. John Paul II, *Lord and Giver of Life,* para. 50.

2. John Paul II, para. 52.

3. John Paul II, para. 7.

4. John Paul II, para. 11.

5. Primarily I have been influenced by the thought of Karl Rahner, especially *The Foundation of the Christian Religion.* A fine summary — and simplification — of his thought on Jesus can be found in Elizabeth Johnson's *Consider Jesus* (New York: Crossroad, 1988). Also helpful was John Haughey's *The Conspiracy of God: The Role of the Holy Spirit* (Mahwah: Paulist Press, 1978).

6. "Pastoral Constitution on the Church in the Modern World," para. 22.

7. I recommend Thomas Keating's *Open Mind, Open Heart* (Rockport: Element, 1989) for an introduction to a simple form of prayer called Centering Prayer. My relationship with Jesus was helped as I realized I could be with Jesus without talking continually.

8. John Paul II, "On the Christian Meaning of Human Suffering," Apostolic Letter, Feb. 11, 1984, para. 23, as translated in J. Walsh and P. Walsh, ed., *Divine Providence and Human Suffering* (Wilmington: Michael Glazier, 1985), p. 247.

9. I've found much help in understanding my unconscious resistance to grace through readings on enneagram theory. Books about the enneagram attempt to describe the nine personality patterns formed before the age of reason that hinder as well as help our response to the

Spirit. *The Enneagram: A Journey of Self Discovery* (Denville: Dimension Books, 1984) by Beesing, Nogosek and O'Leary is helpful because it focuses almost entirely on these nine patterns of resistance.

10. Thomas Keating, *Invitation to Love: The Way of Christian Contemplation* (Rockport: Element, 1992), p. 17.

## VI. All-Powerful *and* All Loving? A Concluding Reflection

1. The attempt to reconcile an all-powerful and all-loving God with the immensity of the world's suffering is called in theological circles *theodicy.*

2. Nelson Pike, ed., *God and Evil: Readings on the Theological Problem of Evil* (Englewood Cliffs: Prentice Hall, 1964), p. 1.

3. Douglas John Hall, *God and Human Suffering: An Exercise in the Theology of the Cross* (Minneapolis; Augsburg Publishing House, 1986), p. 24. I find Hall the best approach to the problem using a biblical perspective that includes both Old and New Testaments.

4. John Hick, *Evil and the God of Love* (San Francisco: Harper & Row, 1978) and Brian Hebblethwaite, *Evil, Suffering and Religion* (New York: Hawthorn Books, 1976). Hick, though difficult reading, is foundational for all who wish to understand the current discussion. Hebblethwaite, simpler and more readable, is similar to but not identical with Hick. My approach is inspired by both, though not identical with either.

5. Those interested in a brief synopsis of Hick's argumentation along with critical responses should consult *Encountering Evil: Live Options in Theodicy,* Stephen T. Davis, ed. (Atlanta: John Knox Press, 1981), Ch. 2, "An Irenaean Theodicy," by John H. Hick, pp. 39–68.

6. Hebblethwaite, p. 74.

7. S. Paul Schilling, *God and Human Anguish* (Nashville; Abingdon, 1977), p. 163. I recommend Schilling's book for an astute as well as readable approach to theodicy.

8. Hall, p. 57. Ch. 2, "Creation: Suffering as Becoming" gives his full explanation.

9. Hall, p. 60.

10. Hall makes the distinction between "integrative" and "disintegrative suffering" — "suffering which is necessary to creaturely becoming (integrative suffering) and suffering which detracts from life (disintegrative suffering)," pp. 67–68.

11. Schilling, p. 173.

12. Hall, p. 74.

13. An excellent treatment of the impact of these assumptions on the discussion of the problem of evil can be found in Stanley Hauerwas, *Naming the Silences: God, Medicine, and the Problem of Suffering* (Grand Rapids: Eerdmanns Publ. Co., 1990), Ch. 2, "Theology, Theodicy and Medicine." The problem of evil arose when Enlightenment thinkers replaced the traditional faith- and community-centered approach with an atheistic and individualistic rationalism.

14. Schilling, p. 181.

15. Schilling, pp. 181–182.

16. *Lord and Giver of Life,* paragraph 12.

17. Hall, p. 118.

18. Hall, p. 79.

19. An extended discussion of this point can be found in Jurgen Moltmann, *The Crucified God* (New York: Harper & Row, 1974), Ch. 6, "The 'Crucified God,'" pp. 200–290, especially pp. 267–290.

20. Schilling, p. 249.

21. Schilling, p. 254.

22. Schilling, p. 235.

23. The full text of the poem is found in many anthologies. W.H. Gardner and N.H. MacKenzie, ed., have compiled the definitive edition of Hopkins' poetry, *The Poems of Gerard Manley Hopkins: Fourth Edition* (New York: Oxford University Press, 1990).